Lean Python

Learn Just Enough Python
to Build Useful Tools

Paul Gerrard

Apress®

Lean Python: Learn Just Enough Python to Build Useful Tools

Paul Gerrard
Maidenhead, Berkshire, United Kingdom

ISBN-13 (pbk): 978-1-4842-2384-0   ISBN-13 (electronic): 978-1-4842-2385-7
DOI 10.1007/978-1-4842-2385-7

Library of Congress Control Number: 2016958723

Managing Director: Welmoed Spahr
Lead Editor: Steve Anglin
Technical Reviewer: Michael Thomas
Editorial Board: Steve Anglin, Pramila Balan, Laura Berendson, Aaron Black, Louise Corrigan, Jonathan Gennick, Robert Hutchinson, Celestin Suresh John, Nikhil Karkal, James Markham, Susan McDermott, Matthew Moodie, Natalie Pao, Gwenan Spearing
Coordinating Editor: Mark Powers
Copy Editor: Teresa F. Horton
Compositor: SPi Global
Indexer: SPi Global
Artist: SPi Global

Distributed to the book trade worldwide by Springer Science+Business Media New York, 233 Spring Street, 6th Floor, New York, NY 10013. Phone 1-800-SPRINGER, fax (201) 348-4505, e-mail orders-ny@springer-sbm.com, or visit www.springeronline.com. Apress Media, LLC is a California LLC and the sole member (owner) is Springer Science + Business Media Finance Inc (SSBM Finance Inc). SSBM Finance Inc is a **Delaware** corporation.

For information on translations, please e-mail rights@apress.com, or visit www.apress.com.

Apress and friends of ED books may be purchased in bulk for academic, corporate, or promotional use. eBook versions and licenses are also available for most titles. For more information, reference our Special Bulk Sales–eBook Licensing web page at www.apress.com/bulk-sales.

Any source code or other supplementary materials referenced by the author in this text are available to readers at www.apress.com. For detailed information about how to locate your book's source code, go to www.apress.com/source-code/. Readers can also access source code at SpringerLink in the Supplementary Material section for each chapter.

Printed on acid-free paper

Contents at a Glance

Contents

About the Author

Paul Gerrard is a consultant, teacher, author, webmaster, programmer, tester, conference speaker, rowing coach, and publisher. He has conducted consulting assignments in all aspects of software testing and quality assurance, specializing in test assurance. He has presented keynote talks and tutorials at testing conferences across Europe, the United States, Australia, and South Africa, and he has occasionally won awards for them.

Educated at the universities of Oxford and Imperial College London, he is a Principal of Gerrard Consulting Limited, the host of the UK Test Management Forum, and the Programme Chair for the 2014 EuroSTAR testing conference.

In 2010 he won the EuroSTAR Testing Excellence Award and in 2013 he won the inaugural TESTA Lifetime Achievement Award.

He has been programming since the mid-1970s and loves using the Python programming language.

About the Technical Reviewer

 **Michael Thomas** has worked in software development for more than 20 years as an individual contributor, team lead, program manager, and vice president of engineering. Michael has more than 10 years of experience working with mobile devices. His current focus is in the medical sector, using mobile devices to accelerate information transfer between patients and health care providers.

Preface

My first exposure to computer programming was at school nearly 40 years ago. My math teacher was a fan of computing and he established the first A-Level Computer Science course in the sixth form college. I didn't take the CS A-Level, as I was committed to Math, Physics, and Chemistry. But my math teacher invited all the scientists to do an informal class in programming, once a week, after hours. It sounded interesting, so I enrolled.

We were introduced to a programming language called CESIL,[1] CESIL a cut-down version of an Assembler language[2] with instructions that had more meaningful names like LOAD, STORE, ADD, and JUMP. We were given green cards on which the instructions and numbers were printed. Next to each instruction was a small oval shape. Beyond that, there was a shape for every letter and numeric value.

Filling in the shapes with a pencil indicated the instructions and data we wanted to use. To make the "job," work we topped and tailed our card deck with some standard instructions on more cards.

Our card decks were secured with rubber bands and sent off to Manchester University for processing. A week later, we usually (but not always) got our cards back together with a printout of the results. If we were lucky, our trivial programs generated some results. More often, our programs did not work, or did not even compile; that is, the computer did not understand our stumbling attempts to write meaningful program code.

I can't remember what programs I wrote in those days. Probably calculating squares of integers or factorials or if I was really ambitious, the sine of an angle using Taylor series. Looping (and more often, infinite looping) was a wonderful feature that had to be taken advantage of. Doing something that simply could not be done by humans was fascinating to me.

The challenge of thinking like the computer and of treating the mysterious machine in Manchester as an infallible wizard that must be obeyed—or at least communicated with in its own pedantic, arcane language—sticks in my mind. You could, with some practice, treat the wizard as your very own tireless slave. Those after-hours classes were great and I looked forward to them every week.

Programming was great fun, if you had a certain interest in control, procedure, and systematic thinking. Nearly 40 years later, I still enjoy battling with code. My programming language of choice nowadays is Python.[3]

---

[1] Computer Education in Schools Instruction Language (see http://en.wikipedia.org/wiki/Cesil). If you are curious, you can download a fully working CESIL interpreter [18].
[2] Assembler is a very low-level language close to actual machine code.
[3] Throughout the book, I use the term Python as shorthand for "the Python programming language."

Introducing Python

The Python programming language was created by Dutchman Guido van Rossum in the late 1980s [1]. Here is a concise summary of Python from Wikipedia [2]:

> *Python is a widely used, general-purpose, high-level programming language. Its design philosophy emphasizes code readability, and its syntax allows programmers to express concepts in fewer lines of code than would be possible in languages such as C. The language provides constructs intended to enable clear programs on both a small and large scale.*

If you choose to learn Python as your first or your 15th programming language, you are making an excellent choice.

Of all the languages I have used (and I think it is about 15, over the years) Python is my favorite. I can't say exactly why, and I don't pretend to be an expert in these matters, but here are some of the things I like about Python:

- Programs are not cluttered up with braces ({...}) and semicolons (;).

- Python implements structure using indentation (white space) rather than punctuation.

- The Python keywords are powerful, limited in number, and do what you expect them to do.

- If you can't work out a way to do something in your code, there is always a library somewhere that does it for you.

- You can get an awful lot done with a limited knowledge of the language'

It is this last feature that I like the most.

Lean Python

I freely admit that I don't know all the features of this wonderful language by heart. In that way, I am a less-than-perfect programmer and I beat myself up about it regularly. I have written about 40,000 lines of Python in the past five years, but I discovered recently that actually, I only need a distinct subset of the language to get things done. I do use all the core elements of the language, of course—lists, dictionaries, objects, and so on—but I don't (and can't) memorize all of the standard functions for each element. I haven't needed them.

I'm looking at a list of the functions and methods for sequences. There are 58 listed in my main Python source book [13]. I have only used 15 of them; I haven't found a need for the rest.

I call this subset *Lean Python* and it is all you need to know as a beginner and some way beyond.

■ **Note**   Lean Python is not "the best way to write code." I offer it as a way of learning the essential aspects of the language without cluttering up your mind with features you might never use.

Now, the code I have written with the Lean Python subset of language features means that on occasion, I have written less optimal code. For example, I discovered only recently that there is a reverse() function that provides a list in reverse order. Of course there is, and why wouldn't there be? Needless to say, I had overlooked this neat feature and have written code to access list elements in reverse order more than once.

These things happen to all programmers. In general, we don't consult the manual unless we have to, so it's a good idea, every now and then, to review the standard list of features for the language to see what might be useful in the future.

Beyond Lean Python

There are many excellent resources available that provide more comprehensive content than this little book. Web sites I would recommend as essential include these:

- python.org. This is the official site for the Python language, and often the best starting point.

- docs.python.org. This site provides the definitive documentation of the standard Python libraries.

There are several excellent sites that offer free, online tutorials. Of course, I also have my own; visit leanpy.com to access it.

Regarding books, there are three that sit on a shelf right above my desk at all times:

- *Core Python Programming,* by Wesley Chun

- *The Python Standard Library by Example,* by Doug Hellmann

- *Python Cookbook,* by Alex Martelli, Anna Ravenscroft, and David Ascher

There are many other excellent books, and you might find better ones, but these are the three that I use myself.

Code Examples in the Book

In this book, you will see quite a lot of example code. Early on you'll see some small code fragments with some narrative text. All code listings are presented in the Courier New font. The shaded text is the code, the unshaded text to the right provides some explanation.

```
#                                    Some explanation appears on the
# some comments and code # in here   right-hand side.
#
myName = 'Paul'
myAge = 21 # if only
```

Later on you'll see longer listings and whole programs. These appear in the book as shaded areas. Some listings have line numbers on the left for reference, but the line numbers are not part of the program code. For example:

```
1   def len(seq):
2       if type(seq) in [list,dict]:  # is it a seq?
3               return -1             # if not, fail!
4       nelems=0                      # length is zero
5       for elem in seq:              # for each elem
6           nelems+=1                 # +1 to length
7
8       return nelems                 # return length
```

There are also some examples of interactions with the Python command-line shell. The shell gives you the >>> prompt. Here's an example:

```
>>> type(23)
<type 'int'>
>>> type('some text')
<type 'str'>
>>> c=[1,2,'some more text']
>>> type(c)
<type 'list'>
```

The lines are not numbered. The lines without the >>> prompt are the outputs printed by the shell.

■ **Note**   Use the code fragments in the shaded sections to practice in the interactive interpreter or run the programs for yourself.

Target Audience

This book is aimed at three categories of readers:

- *The experienced programmer*: If you already know a programming language, this book gives you a shortcut to understanding the Python language and some of its design philosophy.

- *You work in IT and need a programming primer*: You might be a tester who needs to have more informed technical discussions with programmers. Working through the examples will help you to appreciate the challenge of good programming.

- *First-timer*: You want a first book on programming that you can assimilate quickly to help you decide whether programming is for you.

If you require a full-fat, 1,000-page reference book for the Python language, this book is not for you. If you require a primer, appetizer, or basic reference, this book should satisfy your needs.

What This Book Is

This little book provides a sequential learning guide to a useful and usable subset of the Python programming language. Its scope and content are deliberately limited and based on my own experience of using Python to build interactive web sites (using the Web2py web development framework [3]) and many command-line utilities.

This book accompanies the one- and two-day programming courses that I created to help people grasp the basics of a programming language quickly. It isn't a full language reference book, but a reference for people in the course and for whom the Lean Python subset is enough (at least initially).

What This Book Is Not

This book is not intended to be a definitive guide to Python.

Code Comprehension

The initial motivation for writing this book was to help provide nontechnical (i.e., nonprogrammer) testers with an appreciation of programming so they could work more closely with the professional programmers on their teams. Critical to this is the skill I call *code comprehension*, which is your ability to read and understand program code.

Like spoken and written languages, it is usually easier to comprehend written language than write it from scratch. If the book helps you to appreciate and understand written program code, then the book will have succeeded in its first goal.

Python Style Guidelines

One of the most important attributes of code is that it is written to be read by people, not just computers. The Python community gives this goal a high priority. In your own company, you might already have programming or Python guidelines; the Python team have provided some that are widely used [4].

I have tried to follow the guidelines in the sample code and programs. However, in the pocket book format, there is less horizontal space, so sometimes I have had to squeeze code a little to fit it on the page. I tend to use mixed case, e.g., `addTwoNumbers` in my variable and function names.[4]

Some of my code comments, particularly in the early pages, are there to explain what, for example, an assignment does. You would not normally expect to see such "stating the obvious" comments in real code.

"Pythonistas" take the readability goal seriously, and so should you.

There is also a set of design principles you might consult. The Zen of Python sets them out [5]. I'm sure I could have written better examples; if you see an opportunity to improve readability or design, let me know.

Structure

The first seven chapters cover the core features of Python. The later chapters introduce some key libraries and how you can use them to write useful applications.

Chapter 1 introduces the interpreter, the basic syntax of the language, the normal layout, and the conventions of Python. Chapter 2 describes the core Python objects that you will use and need to understand. Chapter 3 sets out how programs are structured and controlled using decisions and loops. Chapter 4 tells you how to get data into and out of your programs with the command line, display, and disk files. Chapter 5 introduces modules that help you to manage your own code and access the thousands of existing libraries. Chapter 6 gives you a flavor for object orientation. Objects and classes are the key building blocks that programmers use. Chapter 7 presents methods for trapping errors and exceptions to allow your programs to be "under control" whatever happens.

Chapter 8 describes how you can use the `unittest` framework to test your code in a professional manner. Chapter 9 introduces libraries allowing you to create a web client and download pages from web sites. Chapter 10 presents regular expressions as the mechanism for more sophisticated searching and pattern-matching. Chapter 11 gives you techniques for creating and using the SQLite relational database for persistent storage. Chapter 12 asks "What Next?" and offers some suggestions for further development of your Python programming skills.

An Appendix contains references to web sites, books and tools, and the Python exception hierarchy. An index is included at the end of the book.

Using Python
Downloading Python

All Python downloads can be found at `https://www.python.org/downloads/`.

You need to choose a Python version before you download. There are currently two versions:

- Version 2 is coming to the end of its life but is still widely used.

- Version 3 has been around for some time; people have been slow to convert but it is gaining a following.

---

[4]The guideline suggests `lower_case_with_underscores`.

The example code in this book assumes you are using Version 3. If you use Python Version 2 you will notice a few differences. You can read a discussion of the two Python versions in [6].

Sample Programs Download

Downloadable sample programs can be found at http://leanpy.com/?page_id=37.

All the sample programs have been tested on Windows 8, Ubuntu Linux 13, and my trusty Raspberry Pi running Linux. If you use a Mac, you should not have problems.

External Libraries

A major benefit to using Python is the enormous range of free libraries that are available for use. The vast majority of these libraries can be found on the PyPI site [7]. When I last looked, there were 46,554 packaged libraries hosted there.

Depending on your operating system (Windows, Mac or Linux), there are several ways of performing installations of Python libraries. The one I find easiest to use is the PIP installer [19] which works nicely with the PyPI site.

Editing Your Python Code

I recommend using either a language-sensitive editor or the editor that comes with your Python installation.

- On Windows, use the IDLE Integrated Development Environment (IDE) or perhaps Notepad++.

- On Linux, there is a selection of editors— vi, vim, emacs, gedit, and so on; I use gedit.

- On OS X, TextMate works fine, but there are other options.

When you are more experienced, you might upgrade to using an IDE. There is a list of Python-compatible IDEs available at https://wiki.python.org/moin/IntegratedDevelopmentEnvironments.

Feedback, Please!

I am very keen to receive your feedback and experience to enhance the format and content of the book. Give me feedback and I'll acknowledge you in the next edition.

Any errors or omissions are my fault entirely. Please let me know how I can improve this book. E-mail me at paul@gerrardconsulting.com with suggestions or errors.

Downloads, errata, further information, and a reading list can be found on the book's web site at leanpy.com.

Acknowledgments

For their helpful feedback, guidance, and encouraging comments, I'd like to thank James Lyndsay, Corey Goldberg, Simon Knight, Neil Studd, Srinivas Kadiyala, Julian Harty, and Fahad Ahmed.

"Everyone knows that debugging is twice as hard as writing a program in the first place. So if you're as clever as you can be when you write it, how will you ever debug it?"

—Brian W. Kernighan

"Talk is cheap. Show me the code"

—Linus Torvalds

"Programs must be written for people to read, and only incidentally for machines to execute"

—Abelson/Sussman

"First, solve the problem. Then, write the code"

—John Johnson

"Sometimes it pays to stay in bed on Monday, rather than spending the rest of the week debugging Monday's code"

—Dan Salomon

"This project is seriously ahead of schedule"

—Perplexed IT director

"The most disastrous thing that you can ever learn is your first programming language"

—Alan Kay

CHAPTER 1

Getting Started

The Python Interpreter

The Python interpreter is a program that reads Python program statements and executes them immediately (see [8] for full documentation). To use the interpreter, you need to open a terminal window or command prompt on your workstation. The interpreter operates in two modes.[1]

Interactive Mode

You can use the interpreter as an interactive tool. In interactive mode, you run the Python program and you will see a new prompt, >>>, and you can then enter Python statements one by one. In Microsoft Windows, you might see something like this:

```
C:\Users\Paul>python
Python 3.4.3 (v3.4.3:9b73f1c3e601, Feb 24 2015, 22:43:06) [MSC v.1600 32 bit
(Intel)] on win32
Type "help", "copyright", "credits" or "license" for more information.
>>> _
```

The interpreter executes program statements immediately. Interactive mode is really useful when you want to experiment or try things out. For example, sometimes you need to see how a particular function (that you haven't used before) behaves. On other occasions, you might need to see exactly what a piece of failing code does in isolation.

---

[1]There are a number of flags and options you can use with the interpreter, but we won't need them.

Electronic supplementary material The online version of this chapter (doi:10.1007/978-1-4842-2385-7_1) contains supplementary material, which is available to authorized users.

© Paul Gerrard 2016
P. Gerrard, *Lean Python*, DOI 10.1007/978-1-4842-2385-7_1

The >>> prompt can be used to enter one-line commands or code blocks that define classes or functions (discussed later). Some example commands are shown here:

```
1  >>> dir(print)
2  ['__call__', '__class__', '__delattr__', '__dir__', '__doc__', '__eq__',
   '__format__', '__ge__', '__getattribute__', '__gt__', '__hash__',
   '__init__', '__le__', '__lt__', '__module__','__name__','__ne__',
   '__new__', '__qualname__', '__reduce__', '__reduce_ex__', '__repr__',
   '__self__', '__setattr__', '__sizeof__', '__str__', '__subclasshook__',
   '__text_signature__']
3  >>>
4  >>> 123.456 + 987.654
5  1111.11
6  >>>
7  >>> 'This'+'is'+'a'+'joined'+'up'+'string.'
8  'Thisisajoinedupstring.'
9  >>>
10 >>> len('Thisisajoinedupstring.')
11 22
```

The dir() command on line 1 lists all the attributes of an object, helpful if you need to know what you can do with an object type. dir() run without an argument tells you what modules you have available. dir(print) shows a list of all the built-in methods for print(), most of which you'll never need.

If you type an expression value, as on line 4, 123.456 + 987.654 the interpreter will execute the calculation and provide the result. The expression on line 7 joins the strings of characters into one long string. The len() function on line 10 gives you the length of a string in characters.

If you define a new function[2] in interactive mode, the interpreter prompts you to complete the definition and will treat a blank line as the end of the function.

```
1  >>> def addTwoNumbers(a,b):
2  ...        result = a + b
3  ...        return result
4  ...
5  >>> addTwoNumbers(3,6)
6  9
7  >>>
```

Note that when the interpreter expects more code to be supplied in a function, for example, it prints the ellipsis prompt (...). In the case of function definitions, a blank line (see line 4 above) completes the function definition.

We define the function in lines 1 through 3 (note the indentation), and the blank line 4 ends the definition. We call the function on line 5 and add 6 + 3, and the result is (correctly) 9.

---

[2]We cover these later, of course.

One other feature of the interactive interpreter is the help() function. You can use this to see the documentation of built-in keywords and functions. For example:

```
>>> help(open)
Help on built-in function open in module io:

open(...)
    open(file, mode='r', buffering=-1, encoding=None, errors=None,
newline=None, closefd=True, opener=None) -> file object

... etc. etc.
```

■ **Note**   The Python interactive interpreter is really handy to try things out and explore features of the language.

Command-Line Mode

In command-line mode, the Python program is still run at the command line but you add the name of a file (that contains your program) to the command:

```
python myprogram.py
```

The interpreter reads the contents of the file (myprogram.py in this case), scans and validates the code, compiles the program, and then executes the program. If the interpreter encounters a fault in the syntax of your program, it will report a compilation error. If the program fails during execution, you will see a runtime error. If the program executes successfully, you will see the output(s) of the program.

You don't need to worry about how the interpreter does what it does, but you do need to be familiar with the types of error messages it produces.

We use command-line mode to execute our programs in files.

Coding, Testing and Debugging Python Programs

The normal sequence of steps when creating a new program is as follows:

1. Create a new .py file that will contain the Python program (sometimes called source code).

2. Edit your .py file to create new code (or amend existing code) and save the file.

3. Run your program at the command prompt to test it, and interpret the outcome.

4. If the program does not work as required, or you need to add more features, figure out what changes are required and go to Step 2.

It's usually a good idea to document your code with comments. This is part of the editing process, Step 2. If you need to make changes to a working program, again, you start at Step 2.

Writing new programs is often called *coding*. When your programs don't work properly, getting programs to do exactly what you want them to do is often called *debugging*.

Comments, Code Blocks, and Indentation

Python, like all programming languages has conventions that we must follow. Some programming languages use punctuation such as braces ({}) and semicolons (;) to structure code blocks. Python is somewhat different (and easier on the eye) because it uses white space and indentation to define code structure.[3] Sometimes code needs a little explanation, so we use comments to help readers of the code (including you) understand it.

We introduce indentation and comments with some examples.

`#`
`# some text after hashes`
`#`
 	
`brdr = 2 # thick border`
	Any text that appears after a hash character (#) is ignored by the interpreter and treated as a comment. We use comments to provide documentation.

`def my_func(a, b, c):`
`    d = a + b + c`
`    ...`
`    ...`
	The colon character (:) denotes the end of a header line that demarks a code block. The statements that follow the header line should be indented.

`if this_var==23:`
`    doThis()`
`    doThat()`
`    ...`
`else:`
`    do_other()`
`    ...`
	Colons are most often used at the end of `if`, `elif`, `else`, `while`, and `for` statements, and function definitions (that start with the `def` keyword).

`def addTwoNumbers(a, b):`
`    "adds two numbers"`
`    return a + b`
	In this example the text in quotes is a docsctring. This text is what a `help(addTwoNumbers)` command would display in the interactive interpreter.

`if long_var is True && \`
`    middle==10 && \`
`    small_var is False:`
`    ...`
`    ...`
	The backslash character (\) at the end of the line indicates that the statement extends onto the next line. Some very long statements might extend over several lines.

(continued)

---

[3]Python 3 disallows mixed spaces and tabs, by the way (unlike version 2).

```xxxxxxxxxxxxxx:` ` xxxxxxxxxxxx` ` xxxxxxxxxxxx` ` xxxxxxxxxxxx` `xxxxxxxxx:` ` xxxxxxxxxxx:` ` xxxxxxx` ` xxxxxxxxxxx:` ` xxxx` ` xxxx```	All code blocks are indented once a header line with a colon appears. All the statements in that block must have the same indentation. Code blocks can be nested within each other, with the same rule: All code in a block has the same indentation. Indentation is most often achieved using four-space increments.
```a = b + c ; p = q + r`  `a = b + c` `p = q + r```	The semicolon character (;) can be used to join multiple statements in a single line. The first line is equivalent to the two lines that follow it.

Variables

A *variable* is a named location in the program's memory that can be used to store some data. There are some rules for naming variables:

- The first character must be a letter or underscore (_).

- Additional characters may be alphanumeric or underscore.

- Names are case-sensitive.

Common Assignment Operations

When you store data in a variable it is called *assignment.* An assignment statement places a value or the result of an expression into variable(s). The general format of an assignment is:

```
var = expression
```

An expression could be a literal, a calculation, a call to a function, or a combination of all three. Some expressions generate a list of values; for example:

```
var1, var2, var3 = expression
```

Here are some more examples:

```
>>> # 3 into integer myint
>>> myint = 3
>>>
>>> # a string of characters into a string variable
>>> text = 'Some text'
```

5

```
>>> # a floating point number
>>> cost = 3 * 123.45
>>> # a longer string
>>> Name = 'Mr' + ' ' + 'Fred' + ' ' + 'Bloggs'
>>> # a list
>>> shoppingList = ['ham','eggs','mushrooms']
>>> # multiple assignment (a=1, b=2, b=3)
>>> a, b, c = 1, 2, 3
```

Other Assignment Operations

Augmented assignment provides a slightly shorter notation, where a variable has its value adjusted in some way.

This assignment	Is equivalent to
x+=1	x = x + 1
x-=23	x = x - 23
x/=6	x = x / 6
x*=2.3	x = x * 2.3

Multiple assignment provides a slightly shorter notation, where several variables are given the same value at once.

This assignment	Is equivalent to
a = b = c = 1	a = 1
	b = 1
	c = 1

So-called multuple assignment provides a slightly shorter notation, where several variables are given their values at once.

This assignment	Explanation
x, y, z = 99, 100, 'OK'	Results in: x=99, y= 100, and z='OK'
p, q, r = myFunc()	If myFunc() returns three values, p, q, and r are assigned those three values.

Python Keywords

Like all programming languages, in Python, some words have defined meanings and are reserved for the Python interpreter. You must not use these words as variable names. Note that they are all lowercase.

and	as	assert	break
class	continue	def	del
elif	else	except	exec
finally	for	from	global
if	import	in	is
lambda	not	or	pass
print	raise	return	try
while	with	yield	

There are a large number of built-in names that you must not use, except for their intended purpose. The cases of True, False, and None are important. The most common ones are listed here.

True	False	None	abs
all	any	chr	dict
dir	eval	exit	file
float	format	input	int
max	min	next	object
open	print	quit	range
round	set	str	sum
tuple	type	vars	zip

To see a list of these built-ins, list the contents of the __builtins__ module in the shell like this:

```
>>> dir(__builtins__)
```

Special Identifiers

Python also provides some special identifiers that use underscores. Their name will be of the form:

```
_xxx
__xxx__
__xxx
```

Mostly, you can ignore these.[4] However, one that you might encounter in your programming is the special system variable:

```
__name__
```

This variable specifies how the module was called. __name__ contains:

- The name of the module if imported.

- The string '__main__' if executed directly.

You often see the following code at the bottom of modules. The interpreter loads your program and runs it if necessary.

```
if __name__ == '__main__':
    main()
```

Python Modules

Python code is usually stored in text files that are read by the Python interpreter at runtime. Often, programs get so large that it makes sense to split them into smaller ones called *modules*. One module can be imported into others using the import statement.

```
import othermod      # makes the code in othermod
import mymodule      # and mymodule available
```

Typical Program Structure

The same program or module structure appears again and again, so you should try and follow it. In this way, you know what to expect from other programmers and they will know what to expect from you.

`#!/usr/bin/python`	Used only in Linux/Unix environments (tells the shell where to find the Python program).

`#`
`# this module does`
`# interesting things like`
`# calculate salaries`
`#`
	Modules should have some explanatory text describing or documenting their behavior.

(continued)

---

[4]The only ones you really need to know are the __name__ variable and the __init__() method called when a new object is created. Don't start your variable names with an underscore and you'll be fine.

```from datetime import datetime```	Module imports come first so their content can be used later in the module.
```now = datetime.now()```	Create a global variable that is accessible to all classes and functions in the module.
```class bookClass(object):` ` "Book object"` ` def __init__(self,title):` ` self.title=title` ` return```	Class definitions appear first. Code that imports this module can then use these classes.
```def testbook():` ` "testing testing..."` ` title="How to test Py"` ` book=bookClass(title)` ` print("Tested the book")```	Functions are defined next. When imported, functions are accessed as `module.function()`.
```if __name__=='__main__':` ` testBook()```	If imported, the module defines classes and functions. If this module is run, the code here (e.g., `testBook()`) is executed.

CHAPTER 2

Python Objects

Every variable in Python is actually an object. You don't have to write object-oriented (OO) code to use Python, but the way Python is constructed encourages an OO approach.[1]

Object Types

All variables have a type that can be seen by using the built-in **type()** function.

```
>>> type(23)
<type 'int'>
>>> type('some more text')
<type 'str'>
>>> c=[1,2,'some more text']
>>> type(c)
<type 'list'>
```

Other types are 'class', 'module', 'function', 'file', 'bool', 'NoneType', and 'long'.
The special constants True and False are 'bool' types. The special constant None is a 'NoneType'.
To see a textual definition of any object, you can use the str() function; for example, the variable c can be represented as a string:

```
>>> str(c)
"[1,2,'some text']"
```

Factory Functions

There are a series of functions that create variable types directly. Here are the most commonly used ones.

---

[1]We introduce object orientation in Chapter 6.

© Paul Gerrard 2016
P. Gerrard, *Lean Python*, DOI 10.1007/978-1-4842-2385-7_2

`int(4.0)`	Creates integer 4
`str(4)`	Creates string '4'
`list(1, 2, 3, 4)`	Creates list [1,2,3,4]
`tuple(1, 2, 3, 4)`	Creates tuple (1,2,3,4)
`dict(one=1, two=2)`	Creates dictionary {'one':1,'two':2}

Numbers

Integer numbers have no realistic limit; you can store and manipulate numbers with 1,000 digits, for example. These are stored as "long" numbers, for example:

```
>>> 12345678901234567890
12345678901234567890
```

Real numbers (i.e., those with decimal points) are stored with what is called double-precision. For example:

```
>>>1 / 7.0
0.14285714285714285
```

The actual degree of precision depends on the architecture of the hardware you use. Very large or very small real numbers can be described using scientific notation.

```
>>> x = 1E20
>>> x / 7.0
1.4285714285714285e+19
>>> int(x/7.0)
14285714285714285714286592
>>> y = 1E-20
>>> y / 7.0
1.4285714285714285e-21
```

Arithmetic Operators

The four arithmetic operators work as expected.

```
# Addition              # Integer 5
2 + 3                   # Real 5.0 (if one or more operands
2.0 + 3                 # are real)

# Subtraction           # Integer 1
3 - 2                   # Real 1.0
3.0 - 2                 # Integer 6

# Multiplication        # Real 6.0
3 * 2                   # Real 6.0
3 * 2.0
3.0 * 2.0

# Division              All divisions produce real numbers
3 / 2                   # 1.5
-6 / 2                  # -3.0
-6 / 4                  # -1.5
3 / 2.0                 # 1.3
```

Other Operators

```
# Modulus               # Real 3.0 (remainder after
15 % 4                  # dividing 15 by 4)

# Exponentiation        # Integer 64
4 ** 3                  # Integer -64 (the '-' applies to
-4 ** 3                 # the result)

                        # Real 0.015625 (NB negative
4 ** -3                 # exponents force operand to real
                        # numbers
```

Conversion Functions

```
int(1.234)              # Integer 1
int(-1.234)             # Integer -1
long(1.234)             # Long 1L
long(-1.234)            # Long -1L
long('1234')            # Long 1234L
long('1.234')           # ** error ** needs 2

long(float('1.234'))    # conversions
                        # Long 1L (after two

float(4)                # conversions)
float('4.321')          # Real 4.0
                        # Real 4.321
```

Boolean Numbers

Booleans are actually held as integers but have a value of either True or False.

```
bool(23)                # True  - all nonzero integers
                        # False - zero

bool(0)                 # True - any string
bool('any text')        # False - zero length strings
bool('')                # False - empty lists
bool([])
```

Random Numbers

Two random number generators are useful (you need to import the random module).

```
import random

random.randint(a,b)     # Generates a random integer
                        # between a and b inclusive.

random.random()

                        # Generates a random real
                        # number between 0.0 and 1.0
```

Sequences: Strings, Lists, and Tuples

So far, we have looked at variables that hold a single value. A *sequence* is a variable that holds multiple values as an array. Each element can be addressed by its position in the sequence as an offset from the first element. The three types of sequence are as follows:

- *Strings*: A sequence of characters that together form a text string.

- *Lists*: A sequence of values where each value can be accessed using an offset from the first entry in the list.

- *Tuples*: A sequence of values, very much like a list, but the entries in a tuple are immutable; they cannot be changed.

We'll look at the Python features that are common to all sequences and then look at the three types separately.

Sequence Storage and Access

The elements of a sequence are stored as a contiguous series of memory locations. The first element in the sequence can be accessed at position 0 and the last element at position $n - 1$ where n is the number of elements in the sequence (see Figure 2-1).

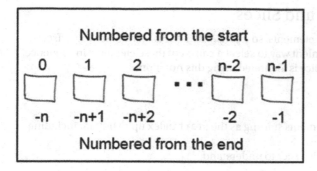

Figure 2-1. *Storage of elements of a sequence*

You can iterate through the elements of a sequence x having n elements starting at element x[0] and adding +1 each time x[1], x[2] ... x[n-1], and so on. You can also iterate from the end and subtract 1 each time: x[n-1], x[n-2] ... x[0].

Membership

A common check is to determine whether a value exists in a sequence. For example:

```
'a' in 'track'                    # True
9 in [1,2,3,4,5,6]                # False

'x' not in 'next'                 # False
'red' not in ['tan','pink']       # True
```

Concatenation[2]

Two or more sequences can be added together to make longer sequences. The plus sign (+) is used to concatenate strings, lists, or tuples.

```
sequence1 + sequence2             # results in a new sequence
                                  # that appends sequence2 to
                                  # sequence1

'mr'+'joe'+'soap'                 # 'mrjoesoap'
```

---

[2]It is recommended that you use the join() string method to join a list of strings or a tuple, as it is more efficient. For example:

```
>>> '-'.join(('a','b','c','d'))
'a-b-c-d'
```

Sequence Elements and Slices

A sequence is an ordered list of elements, so a single element is identified by its offset from the first. A slice is a convenient way to select a subset of these elements in sequence, producing a new sequence. A slice is identified using this notation:

[startindex:endindex]

The slice will consist of elements starting as the startindex up to but not including endindex.

Some examples will make it easier to understand:

```
mylist=['a','b','c','d','e']    # a list with five
                                # elements
mylist[0]                       # 'a'
mylist[3]                       # 'd'
mylist[5]                       # results in an error
mylist[-1]                      # 'e'
mylist[1:3]                     # ['b','c']
mylist[:4]                      # ['a','b','c']
mylist[3:]                      # ['d','e']
```

Sequences can be nested and elements accessed using multiple indexes, for example:

```
mylist = [1,2,3,['a','b','c'],5]
mylist[2]                # 3
mylist[3]                # ['a','b','c']
mylist[3][1]             # 'b'
```

Sequence Built-In Functions

```
mylist=[4,5,6,7,1,2,3]
len(seq)                  # the length of seq
len(mylist)               # 7
                          # maximum value in seq
max(seq)                  # 7
max(mylist)               # 1 - the minimum
min(mylist)
```

Strings

A *string* is a sequence of characters that make up a piece of text. Strings are immutable, but you can update the value of a string by assigning a new string to the same string variable.

```
>>> mystr = 'Paddington Station'
>>> mystr=mystr.upper()      # replaces mystr
>>> mystr
PADDINGTON STATION
```

Assignment

You can delimit strings with either single (') or double (") quotes, as long as they are matched. You can embed either quote inside the other.

```
>>> text = 'Hello World!'
>>> longtext = "A longer piece of text"
>>> print(text)
Hello World!
>>>longtext
'A longer piece of text'
>>> text = 'Paul said, "Hello World!"'
>>>print(text)
Paul said, "Hello World!"
```

Accessing Substrings

You access substrings with slices, of course:

```
text='Paul said, "Hi"'
text[:4]                        # 'Paul'
text[-4:]                       # '"Hi"'
text[5:9]                       # 'said'
text[0:4] + text[12:14]         # 'PaulHi'
```

String Comparison

Strings can be compared[3] as follows:

```
'mcr'>'liv'                     # True
'liv'>'tot'                     # False
'mcr'=='X'                      # False
'X'>'t'                         # False
```

---

[3]You can see the ASCII collation sequence at http://www.asciitable.com/. Space precedes the numeric characters, which precede the uppercase letters; lowercase letters come last.

17

Membership (Searching)

We can check whether a substring is in a string, character by character or using substrings. The outcome is a Boolean.

```
'a' in 'the task'           # True
'w' in 'the task'           # False
'as' in 'the task'          # True
'job' not in 'the task'     # True
'task' in 'the task'        # True
```

Special Characters and Escaping

A string can contain nonprinting and control characters (e.g., tab, newline, and other special characters) by "escaping" them with a backslash (\). Common escape characters are the following:

```
\0 Null character
\t Horizontal tab
\n Newline character
\' Single quote
\" Double quote
\\ Backslash
```

```
>>> multiline='Line 1\nLine 2\nLine 3'
>>> print(multiline)
Line 1
Line 2
Line 3
```

Triple Quotes

Longer pieces of text with embedded newlines can be assigned using the triple quotes notation; for example:

```
>>> multiline="""Line1
... Line 2
... Line 3"""
>>> multiline
'Line 1\nLine 2\nLine 3'
```

String Formatting

The percent (%) operator provides string formatting functionality. This feature has a structure like this:

formatstring % (arguments to format)

formatstring is a string that contains text to be output with embedded conversion symbols denoted by a percent sign (%). These are the common conversion symbols:

%c	Single character/string of length 1
%s	String
%d	Signed decimal integer
%f	Floating point number
%%	Percent character

Here are some examples:

```
>>> ntoys = 4
>>> myname='Fred'
>>> length = 1234.5678
>>> '%s has %d toys' % (myname,ntoys)
'Fred has 4 toys'
>>> 'is %s playing?' % (myname)
'is Fred playing?'
>>> 'length= %.2f cm' % length
'length= 1234.56 cm'
>>> 'units are %6s meters' % length
```

In the preceding examples, the .2 in %.2f indicates the number of decimal places. The 6 in %6s implies a field width of 6 characters.

String Functions

There are a large number of built-in string functions. The most common ones are illustrated here. Note that these all return a new string; they do not make changes to strings because strings are immutable.

```
text = 'This is text'
nums = '123456'
# finding text

text.find('is')              # returns 2
text.find('your')            # returns -1

# Validation checks          # all alphas? True
text.isalpha()
text.isdigit()               # all digits? False
nums.isdigit()               # True

# concatenation              #'This is text123456'
''.join((text,nums))         #'This is text 123456'
' '.join((text,nums))
                             # 'THIS IS TEXT'
# case changing              # 'this is text'
text.upper()
text.lower()                  # list of strings:
                             #['This','is','text']

# splitting string
text.split(' ')
                             # This was text

# substitution
text.replace('is','was')

                             # remove trailing space
# stripping                  # remove leading space
text.rstrip()
text.lstrip()                # remove trailing and leading spaces
text.strip()
```

Lists

Lists are widely used to store values that are collected and processed in sequence, such as lines of text read from or written to a text file, or where prepared values are looked up by their position or offset in the array.

Creating Lists

```
mylist = []                  # an empty list
names=['Tom','Dick','Harry'] # list of strings
mixedlist = [1,2,3,'four']   # list of mixed
                             # types
elist = [1,2,3,[4,5,6]]      # embedded list
```

You can find the length of lists using the len() function. The length is the number of elements in the list. The last element index of a list mylist would be accessed as mylist[len(mylist)-1].

```
l = len(names)                                          # 3
```

Values in the preceding lists are accessed as shown in the following code fragments.

```
names[1]            # 'Dick'
mixedlist[0]        # 1
mixedlist[3]        # 'four'
mixedlist[2:4]      # [3,'four']
elist[2]            # 3
elist[3]            # [4,5,6]
elist[3][1]         # 5
```

If you try to access a nonexistent element in the list, you will get a 'list index out of range' error.

Updating Lists

Use the append() method to add entries to the end of a list. Use the del statement to delete an entry. For example:

```
mylist = []                  # an empty list
mylist.append('Tom')         # ['Tom']
mylist.append('Dick')        # ['Tom','Dick']
mylist.append('Harry')       # ['Tom','Dick','Harry']

# Change an entry
mylist[1]='Bill'             # ['Tom','Bill','Harry']

# Delete an entry           # ['Tom','Harry']
del mylist[1]
```

Indexing

Whereas the membership (in, not in) operators return a Boolean True or False, the index() method finds an entry in your list and returns the offset of that entry. If the entry cannot be found, it returns an error.

```
mylist=['Tom','Dick','Harry']
mylist.index('Dick')                    # 1
mylist.index('Henry')                   # ValueError: Henry
                                        # not in list
```

Sequence Operations and Functions

The sequence operators—comparisons, slices, membership, and concatenation—all work the same as they do with strings.

The sequence functions—len(), max(), min(), sum(), sorted() and reversed()—all work as expected.

Tuples

Like numbers and strings, tuples are immutable. They are useful for preset lookups or validators you might reuse.

Creating Tuples

To distinguish a tuple from a list, Python uses parentheses () to enclose the entries in a tuple.

```
>>> mynumbers = (1,2,3,4,5,6,7)
>>> months=('Jan','Feb','Mar','Apr','May','Jun',
... 'Jul','Aug','Sep','Oct','Nov','Dec')
>>> mixed = ('a',123,'some text',[1,2,3,'testing'])

# accessing tuples
>>> mynumbers[3]              # 4
>>> months[3:6]              # ('Apr','May','Jun')
>>> mixed[2]+' '+mixed[3][3]   # 'some text testing'
```

You can find the length of tuples using the len() function. The length is the number of elements in the list.

If you try to access a nonexistent element in the list, you will get a 'tuple index out of range' error.

Sequence Operations and Functions

The sequence operators—comparisons, slices, membership, and concatenation—all work as expected. The index() method works exactly as that for lists. The sequence functions—len(), max(), min(), sum(), sorted(), and reversed()—all work as expected.

Dictionaries

If we want our program to remember a collection of values, we can use lists and we can access the entries using the index to those values. To find the value we want, though, we must know the offset to that value (or search for it).

Dictionaries provide a lookup facility based on key/value pairs. The order of the entries in a dictionary is not defined (in fact, it is somewhat random), but every entry can be retrieved by using its key. Keys must be unique; there can only be one entry in a dictionary for each key.

Creating a Dictionary

You can create a dictionary using a set of key/value pairs.

```
>>> # days of week - seven key-value pairs
>>> wdays={'M':'Monday','T':'Tuesday',
... 'W':'Wednesday','Th':'Thursday',
... 'F':'Friday','Sa':'Saturday',
... 'Su':'Sunday'}
>>> wdays['M']
'Monday'
>>> wdays['W']
'Wednesday'
>>> wdays['Su']
'Sunday'

>>> newdict = {}      # empty dictionary
```

Updating a Dictionary

You can update dictionaries using the dict[key] convention.

```
>>> newdict = {}      # empty dictionary


>>> newdict['1st'] = 'first entry' # add 1st entry
>>> newdict['2nd'] = 'second entry'# add 2nd entry
>>> newdict['1st'] = 'new value'   # update 1st entry

>>> del newdict['2nd']             # delete 2nd entry

>>> len(newdict)                   # 1
```

Dictionary Operations

The sequence operators—comparisons, membership, and concatenation—all work as expected. Here are a few dictionary operations that you might find useful:

```
# days of week - seven key/value pairs

# key existence
>>> 'Sa' in wdays
True
>>> 'Sp' in wdays
False
```

23

```
# create list of keys
>>> wdays.keys()
['M','T','W','Th','F','Sa','Su']

# create an iterable list of values
>>> wdays.values()
dict_values(['Monday','Tuesday','Wednesday','Thursday','Friday','Saturday',
'Sunday'])

# look up a key with a default if key not found
>>> wdays.get('X','Not a day')
'Not a day'
```

CHAPTER 3

Program Structure

Decision Making

Some simple utilities might be a short list of statements run in order, but a useful program usually needs to make decisions and choices. The decision making in a program determines the path that the program takes. Decisions are made by if statements.

The if Statement

if statements depend on some form of test or condition. The normal format of an if statement is shown here:

```
if test:             # note the colon ':'.
    statement1       # The statements following the
    statement2       # if are indented and executed
    statement3       # if the test is True.
```

In this case, the three statements are executed if test is True. Otherwise these statements are skipped and the interpreter skips to the statement following the code block.

Often, the False outcome of the test has its own code block, as follows:

```
if test:             # note the colon ':'.
    DoThis()         # DoThis() ... if test=True
else:                # note the colon after 'else'
    DoThat()         # DoThat() ... if test=False
```

The else: keyword separates the True outcome of the test from the False outcome of the test and directs the compiler to take the alternate code block: DoThat().

So far, we've seen a binary decision with only a True and a False outcome. Some if statements make a choice from more than two alternatives. In this case, the elif: keyword separates the different choices and the else: keyword is the final choice if no other test is met. For example:

```
1    If code=='RED':
2        SoundRedAlert()
```

© Paul Gerrard 2016
P. Gerrard, *Lean Python*, DOI 10.1007/978-1-4842-2385-7_3

```
3   elif code=='AMBER':
4       GiveWarning()
5   else:
6       pass
```

■ **Note**   that the indentation of the if and its corresponding elif and else keywords must all be the same.

The pass Statement

In the preceding example, depending on the value of code, the program makes a choice to do something, but the third choice was pass. The pass statement is a "do nothing" statement. The third clause (else) is not strictly necessary, but pass is often useful to show explicitly what the program is doing (or not doing).

Types of Test

The tests that are applied in an if statement can take many forms, but the main patterns are summarized here.

- *Comparisons*

```
var1 > var2      # greater than
var1 == var2     # equal to
var1 != var2     # not equal to
```

- *Sequence (list, tuple, or dictionary) membership*

```
var in seq
var not in seq
```

- *Sequence length*

```
len(x)>0     # sequence has entries?
```

- *Boolean value*

```
fileopen       # fileopen==True?
not fileopen   # fileopen==False?
```

- *Has a value?*

```
var            # not None (or zero or '')
```

- *Validation*

```
var.isalpha()    # alphanumeric?
var.isdigit()    # is all digits?
```

- *Calculations*

```
(price*quantity) > 100.0 # cost>100?
(cost-budget) > 0.0      # overbudget?
```

In the case of calculations it is often better to use braces to force the calculations than to rely on the default operator precedence.

Some decisions are more complex and require multiple tests to implement. For example:

```
if hungry and foodInFridge and notTooTired:
    cookAMeal()
else:
    getTakeAway()
```

In this case, the and operator joins the three conditions and all must be True for cookAMeal() to be executed.

There are three logical operators—and, or, and not—that can be used to link decisions.

Decisions can be nested; that is, they can appear inside the indented code blocks of other decisions. For example:

```
if age>19:
    if carValue>10000:
        if gotConvictions:
            rejectInsuranceApplication()
```

Loops and Iteration

Some features need to perform activities repetitively to process a number of items, including the following:

- Lists of values.

- Entries in a dictionary.

- Rows of data in a database.

- Lines of text in a disk file.

These constructs, usually called *loops*, perform a defined code block repeatedly on some item of data until some condition or test is met (or not met). These loops are implemented using for and while statements.

For Statement

The for statement acts as a header statement for a code block that is to be executed until some condition is met. The for statement operates on an iterable set of elements, often a sequence.

```
>>> theTeam=['Julia','Jane','Tom','Dick','Harry']
>>> for person in theTeam:
...     print('%s is in the team' % person)
Julia is in the team
Jane is in the team
Tom is in the team
Dick is in the team
Harry is in the team
```

The general format is 'for var in seq:'.

For each iteration through the members of the sequence, the variable var takes the value of the entry in the list or tuple, or it takes the value of the key in a dictionary.

Sometimes we don't want to iterate through a list or dictionary, but we want to execute a loop a specific number of times. Python provides a useful range() function that generates an iterable list of specific size for us. It can take three arguments—start, end, and step—that specify the first number, the maximum number, and the increment between elements in the generated range, respectively. If you provide just one number argument, it creates a list with that number of integer elements starting with zero.

```
>>> range(10)
range(0,10)       # a list of ten elements 0-9
>>> range(1,10)   # default step=1
range(1,10)       # list: [1,2,3,4,5,6,7,8,9]
>>> range(1,20,3) # steps of 3
range(1,20,3)     # list: [1,4,7,10,13,16,19]

>>> for i in range(3):
...     print(i)
0
1
2
```

While Statement

The while statement is similar to the for statement in that it provides a header statement for a code block to be repeated a number of times. Instead of an iterable set of elements, the while statement repeats the loop until a test is not met.

```
>>> n=4
>>> while n>0:
...     print(n)
...     n-=1
```

```
4
3
2
1
```

Often, the condition to be met is a counter that is decremented in the loop or a Boolean value the value of which is changed inside the loop, and then the loop is terminated.

```
>>> foundSmith=False
>>> while not foundSmith:
...     name=getNextName()    # get next person record
...     if name=='smith':     # name is 'smith'?
                foundSmith=True
```

Break Statement

A break statement is used to terminate the current loop and continue to the next statement after the for or while code block.

```
1   while True:      # this is an infinite loop
2       command=input('Enter command:')
3       if command=='exit': # infinite till user exits
4           break               # skips to line 7
5       else:
6           doCommand(command) # execute command
7   print('bye')
```

Continue Statement[1]

A continue statement is used in the code block of a loop to exit from the current code block and skip to the next iteration of the loop. The while or for loop test is checked as normal.

```
1   while True:      # this is an infinite loop
2       command=input('Enter command:')
3       if len(command)==0:  # no command - try again
4           continue     # goes to next loop (line 1)
5       elif command=='exit': # user exit
6           print('Goodbye')
7           break        # skips to line 10
8       else:
9           doCommand(command)
10  print('bye')
```

---

[1]In the examples that follow, the doCommand() function needs to be defined, of course.

List Comprehensions

A *list comprehension* (also known as a *listcomp*) is a way of dynamically creating a list of elements in an elegant shorthand. Suppose you wanted to create a list of the squares of the first ten integers. You could use this code:

```
squares=[]
for i in range(1,11):
   squares.append(i*i)
```

Or you could use this:

```
squares=[i*i for i in range(1,11)]
```

The syntax for listcomps is:

```
[expr for element in iterable if condition]
```

The if condition can be used to select elements from the iterable. Here are some examples of this syntax in use:

```
# a list of even numbers between 1 and 100
evens = [i for i in range(1,100) if not i % 2]

# a list of strings in lines containing 'True'
trulines = [l for l in lines if l.find('True')>-1]
```

Using Functions
Why Write Functions?

When you write more complicated programs, you can choose to write them in long, complicated modules, but complicated modules are harder to write and difficult to understand. A better approach is to modularize a complicated program into smaller, simpler, more focused modules and functions.

The main motivation for splitting large programs into modules and functions is to better manage the complexity of the process.

- Modularization "divides and conquers" the complexity into smaller chunks of less complex code, so design is easier.

- Functions that do one thing well are easier to understand and can be very useful to you and other programmers.

- Functions can often be reused in different parts of a system to avoid duplicating code.

- If you want to change some behavior, if it's in a function, you only need to change code in one place.

- Smaller functions are easier to test, debug, and get working.

Importantly, if you choose to use a function written by someone else, you shouldn't need to worry too much how it works, but you need to trust it.[2]

What Is a Function?

A function is a piece of program code that is:

- A self-contained coherent piece of functionality.

- Callable by other programs and modules.

- Passed data using arguments (if required) by the calling module.

- Capable of returning results to its caller (if required).

You already know about quite a few built-in Python functions. One of these is the len() function. We just call len() and pass a sequence as a parameter. We don't need to write our own len() function, but suppose we did write one of our own (for lists and dictionaries only). It might look something like this:

```
>>> def lenDictList(seq):
...     if type(seq) not in [list,dict]: # a seq?
...         return -1                     # no - fail!
...     nelems=0                          # length zero
...     for elem in seq:                  # for elem
...         nelems+=1                     # add one
...
... return nelems                         # length
...
```

The header line has a distinct format:

- The keyword def to signify it is a new function.

- A function name lenDictList (that meets the variable naming rules).

- Braces to enclose the arguments (none, 1 or more).

- A colon to denote the end of the header line.

The code inside the function is indented. The code uses the arguments in the function definitions and does not need to define them (they will be passed by the calling module). Here are some examples:

```
>>> l = [1,2,3,4,5]
>>> d = {1:'one',2:'two',3:'three'}
>>> lenDictList(l)
5
```

---

[2]All open source or free-to-use libraries come with a health warning, but if you see many references to a library on programmer web sites and in books, you can be reasonably confident that it works.

```
>>> lenDictList(d)
3
>>> lenDictList(34)
-1
```

Note that the real len() handles any sequence including tuples and strings and does better error-handling. This is a much oversimplified version.

Return Values

The results of the function are returned to the caller using the return statement. In the preceding example, there is one return value: the length of the list or dictionary provided or it is –1 if the argument is neither.

Some functions do not return a result; they simply exit.

It is for the programmer to choose how to design his or her functions. Here are some example return statements.

```
return                  # does not return a value
return True             # True - perhaps success?
return False            # False - perhaps a failure?
return r1, r2, r3       # returns three results
return dict(a=v1,b=v2)  # returns a dictionary
```

Calling a Function

Functions are called by using their name and adding parentheses enclosing the variables or values to be passed as arguments. You know len() already. The other functions are invented to illustrate how functions are used.

```
>>> count = len(seq)       # length of a sequence
>>>
>>> # the call below returns three results, the
>>> # maximum, the minimum, and the average of
>>> # the numbers in a list
>>> max, min, average = analyse(numlist)
>>>
>>> # the next call provides three parameters
>>> # and the function calculates a fee
>>> fee = calculateFee(hours, rate, taxfactor)
```

■ **Note**   The number of variables on the left of the assignment must match the number of return values provided by the function.

Named Arguments

If a function just has a single argument, then you might not worry what its name is in a function call. Sometimes, though, not all arguments are required to be provided and they can take a default value. In this case you don't have to provide a value for the argument. If you do name some arguments in the function call, then you must provide the named arguments after the unnamed arguments. Here is an example:

```
def fn(a, b, c=1.0):
return a*b*c
fn(1,2,3)              # 1*2*3 = 6
fn(1,2)               # 1*2*1 = 2 - c=default 1.0
fn(1,b=2)             # 1*2*1 = 2 - same result
fn(a=1,b=2,c=3)       # 1*2*3 = 6 - as before
fn(1,b=2,3)           # error! You must provide
                      # named args *after* unnamed
                      # args
```

■ **Note**   In your code, you must define a function before you can call it. A function call must not appear earlier in the code than the definition of that function or you will get an "undefined" error.

Variable Scope

The variables that are defined and used inside a function are not visible or usable to other functions or code outside the function. However, if you define a variable in a module and call a function inside that module, then that variable is available in the called function. If a variable is defined outside all the functions in a module, the variable is available to all of the functions in the module.[3] For example:

```
sharedvar="I'm sharable"   # a var shared by both
                           # functions
def first():
    print(sharedvar)       # this is OK
    firstvar='Not shared'  # this is unique to first
    return

def second():
    print(sharedvar)       # this is OK
    print(firstvar)        # this would fail!
    return
```

---

[3]Sometimes it is convenient to create shared variables that save you time and the hassle of adding them as arguments to the functions in a module. If you use these variables as places to pass data between functions, though, you might find problems that are hard to diagnose. Treating them as readonly variables will reduce the chance of problems that are hard to debug.

33

CHAPTER 4

■ ■ ■

Input and Output

If a program did not produce any output, it wouldn't be very useful, would it? If a program did not accept some data that varied from time to time, it would produce the same result again and again and again, and that wouldn't be very useful either (after its first run at least). Most programs, therefore, need to accept some inputs or input data, so that they can product output data, outputs, or results.

In this chapter, we cover three important input/output mechanisms:

- Displayed output.

- Getting data from the user through the keyboard.

- Getting input from and writing output to disk files.

Displaying Output

You've seen the print() function[1] quite a few times already. The most common way of getting output from a program is to use the print() statement. Print is a function that takes as its arguments the items to be displayed. Optionally, you can also define a separator that is placed between the displayed items and a line terminator value that can replace a newline. The function call looks like this:

```
print(arg1,arg2,arg3...,sep=' ',end='\n')
```

Here are some examples of the print() function in use.

```
>>> boy="Jack"
>>> girl="Jill"
>>> print("Hello World!")
Hello World!
>>> print(boy,'and',girl,'went up the hill')
Jack and Jill went up the hill
```

---

[1]Note that in Version 2, print was a statement, not a function, so it behaves differently. Print() is a common Version 3 stumbling block so take a look at https://docs.python.org/3/whatsnew/3.0.html.

© Paul Gerrard 2016
P. Gerrard, *Lean Python*, DOI 10.1007/978-1-4842-2385-7_4

It is common to use the string formatting feature.

```
>>> print('%d plus %d makes %d' % (3, 7, 10))
3 plus 7 makes 10
```

You can suppress the trailing newline by setting the end argument to an empty string (or something else).

```
>>> #
>>> # the end= argument defaults to '\n'
>>> # if you change it, there won't be a newline
>>> #
>>> print('one...','two...','three',end='')
one... two... three>>>    # note the >>> prompt
```

The string separator defaults to a single space but can be changed or suppressed by setting it to an empty string.

```
>>> #
>>> # the sep= argument defaults to a space ' '
>>> # but you can change it, for example...
>>> #
>>> print('one...','two...','three',sep='***')
one...***two...***three
```

Getting User Input

The easiest way to get data into the program is to use the input()[2] function. It takes one argument, which is the prompt you see displayed on the command line. The function returns a string value, so if you are asking for numeric or multiple values separated by commas, you will have to parse and process the text in the code before the data can be used.

```
>>> yourName=input('Enter your name: ')
Enter your name: Paul
>>> print('Your name is',yourName)
Your name is Paul
```

If you ask the user for an integer number, you should check that the entered text is valid and can be converted to an integer. To do this, you might do the following:

- Use len(text) to verify that some text has been entered.

- Use the string function text.isdigit() to check the text represents a number.

---

[2]In Version 2, Python uses the function raw_input() instead. It works exactly like the input() function in Version 3.

- Use the int(text) to convert the text to an integer so you can process it.

You might have heard of the "garbage-in, garbage-out" concept. If you don't validate the data coming into your program, its behavior might be unpredictable or it might fail or just produce strange results. Don't forget that hackers can exploit poor input validation to cause mayhem on Internet sites.

■ **Note** It is your responsibility, as programmer, to ensure that only data that meets your validation rules is accepted by your program.

Writing and Reading Files

At one point or another, you are going to have to read and write text files on disks or other devices. We look specifically here at text-only files and how you can access them.

Opening Files

To access a file on disk you create a file object and you use the open() function to do this. The format of the open call is:

```
fileobj = open(filename,mode)
```

The named file would normally be opened in the current directory, but the name can include a path so it can open any file on any disk and in any directory (local permissions allowing). The mode tells the interpreter to open the file for reading 'r', writing 'w', or appending 'a'.

Table 4-1 shows the outcomes of opening existing and nonexistent files with the three mode values.

Table 4-1. *Opening Files with the Three Mode Values*

Open Mode	File Exists	File Does Not Exist
'r'	Open for reading	No such file or directory error
'w'	Overwritten by empty file and open for writing	Open for writing
'a'	Open for appending	New empty file created and open for writing

---

■ **Note** Be careful when using the write mode; you might overwrite a file containing valuable data and lose it.

Here are some examples of how to open files:

```
fname='myfile.txt'
fp = open(fname,'r')  # open for reading (must exist)
fp = open(fname,'w')  # creates new file for writing
fp = open(fname,'a')  # opens file for appending
```

Closing Files

Once you have finished reading from or writing to a file, it is a good idea to close it using the close() function.

```
fp = open(fname,'w')  # open for writing
#
# do some writing, etc.
#
fp.close()
```

If you don't explicitly close files, you shouldn't encounter any major problem, but it is always best to pair open() and close() functions for the sake of completeness and tidiness.

Reading Files

The standard function to read data from a file is read(). It reads the entire contents of the file into a string variable. The content can then be split into separate lines delimited by the newline character ('\n').

```
fp = open(fname,'r')  # open for reading
text = fp.read()
lines=text.split('\n')
fp.close()
```

A more common way to read a file into memory is readlines(), which returns a list containing each line.

```
fp = open(fname,'r')  # open for reading
lines = fp.readlines()
fp.close()
```

Every entry in the lines list just shown will have a newline at its end, so a good way of cleaning up the readlines() data would be to use a list comprehension:

```
lines = [line.rstrip() for line in fp.readlines()]
```

If you want to read a file line by line, the best way is to make use of the fact that the file object itself returns an iterator like this:

```
fp = open(fname,'r')   # open for reading
for eachLine in fp:
  #
  # process each line in turn
  #
  print(eachLine,end='')   # suppress the extra \n
fp.close()
```

■ **Note**   Whichever way you read a file, the text that is read contains the trailing newline character; you must remove it yourself.

Writing to Files

The standard function to write data to a file is write(), which works exactly as you would expect.

```
fp.write(textline)
```

Note that the write() function does not append a newline to the text before writing. Here is a simple example:

```
fp = open('text.txt','w')
while True:
    text = input('Enter text (end with blank):')
    if len(text)==0:
        break
    else:
        fp.write(text+'\n')
fp.close()
```

If you didn't add the trailing '\n' newline in the write statement, all the lines of text would be merged into a single long string. If you have a list of strings, you can write the list out as a file in one statement, but you must remember to append a newline to each string to make the file appear as you expect.

Here are two ways of writing out a list to a file:

```
lines=['line 1','line 2','line 3','line 4']

# write all lines with no '\n'
fp.writelines(lines)
```

```
# writes all line with '\n'
fp.writelines([line+'\n' for line in lines])
```

■ **Note** The write() and writelines() functions do not append trailing newline (\n) characters; you must do that yourself.

Accessing the File System

There are a number of useful file system functions. They are all available using the os module, which you must import.

```
import os

# remove a file (deleteme.txt) from disk
os.unlink('deleteme.txt')
# rename file on disk (from file.txt to newname.txt)
os.rename('file.txt','newname.txt')
# change current/working directory
os.chdir(newdirectory)
# create list of files in a directory
filelist = os.listdir(dirname)
# obtain current directory
curdir = os.getcwd()
# create a directory
os.mkdir(dirname)
# remove a directory (requires it to be empty)
os.rmdir(dirname)

# in the following examples, we need to use
# the os.path module
#
# does the file/directory exist?
exists = os.path.exists(path)
# does path name exist and is it a file?
isfile = os.path.isfile(filepathname)
# does path name exist and is it is directory?
isdir = os.path.isdir(filepath)
```

Command-Line Arguments

The input() function allows you to get input from the user using the keyboard at any point in your program. Often, though, it is more convenient to the user to provide input directly after the program name in a command line. Most command-line utilities have options and data to be used in its process; for example:

```
python mycopy.py thisfile.txt thatfile.txt
```

This might be a program that makes a copy of one file to another.

The arguments are captured in the sys.argv list from the sys module. Here is some code that demonstrates how to capture the command-line arguments (command.py):

```
import sys

nargs=len(sys.argv)
print('%d argument(s)' % (nargs))
n=0
for a in sys.argv:
    print('  arg %d is %s' % (n,a))
    n+=1
```

Let's try running our program with three arguments:

```
D:\LeanPython>python command.py arg1 arg2 arg3
4 argument(s)
  arg 0 is command.py
  arg 1 is arg1
  arg 2 is arg2
  arg 3 is arg3
```

Note that the first (element 0) argument is always the name of the program itself.

CHAPTER 5

Using Modules

Once you have more than a hundred (or several hundred) lines of code in one Python file, it can be a little messy to manage all the functions and classes in the same place. Splitting your code over two or more module files that each cover one aspect of the functionality can simplify matters greatly.

The features and functions in the standard library (and other libraries that you might download and use from time to time) are made available to your programs as modules using the import statement.

Whether you are using your own home-grown modules or the standard libraries, the mechanism for including the code is the same.

Importing Code from a Module

The import statement has this format:

```
import modulename [as name]
```

This statement imports the module modulename. The optional 'as name' part allows you to reference that module with a different name in your code. If this statement works without error, then all of the functions and classes in that module are available for use.

Modules Come from the Python Path

When Python encounters an import modulename statement, it looks for a file called modulename.py to load.[1] It doesn't look just anywhere. Python has an internal variable called the Python path. You can see what it is by examining the sys.path variable.

The following interaction shows the path on a Windows machine.

```
>>> import sys
>>> sys.path
['', 'C:\\Windows\\SYSTEM32\\python34.zip', 'c:\\Python34\\DLLs',
'c:\\Python34\\lib', 'c:\\Python34', 'c:\\Python34\\lib\\site-packages']
>>>
```

---

[1]The import statement assumes your module files end with '.py'.

The Python path is a list of directories that is set up by the Python installation process, but you can also access and change the path to suit your circumstances.

When you install other libraries (e.g., from PyPI) the path might be updated. If you keep all your Python code in one place (in the same, current directory), you will never need to change the Python path. You only need to worry about the Python path if you are dealing with many modules in different locations.

Creating and Using Your Own Modules

Let's suppose that you have a module with Python code called mod1.py; the name of the module in your code will be mod1. You also have a program file called testmod.py. Let's look at some example code in each file.

This is mod1.py:

```
def hello():
    print('hello')

writtenby='Paul'

class greeting():
    def morning(self):
        print('Good Morning!')
    def evening(self):
        print('Good Evening!')
```

Now, suppose we have a test program mod1test1.py:

```
import mod1 as m1

print(writtenby)

m1.hello()
print('written by', m1.writtenby)

greet = m1.greeting()
greet.morning()
greet.evening()
```

Now, you can see in line 1 that we have imported mod1 as m1. This means that the code in module mod1 is referenced using the m1 prefix. If we had just imported the module, we would use the prefix mod1. When we run this code, we get the following result:

```
D:\LeanPython\programs>python mod1test1.py
hello
written by Paul
Good Morning!
Good Evening!
```

Let's look at another test file (mod1test2.py).

```
from mod1 import greeting,hello,writtenby

hello()
hello.writtenby='xxx'
print('written by', hello.writtenby)
print(writtenby)

greet = greeting()
greet.morning()
greet.evening()
```

In this case we have imported the function and class using this format:

```
from module import function1, function2…
```

When we run this code, we get the following result:

```
D:\LeanPython\programs>python mod1test2.py
hello
written by xxx
Paul
Good Morning!
Good Evening!
```

You can see that the import format allows us to drop the prefix for the imported functions.

We now import only what we want and we also can name the imported functions and classes without the prefix. We could also have used the format:

```
from module import *
```

In this alternative we import all the functions and classes from the module. The result would have been the same for mod1test2.py; there would be no need for prefixes.

When we import from the standard libraries, which often have a large number of functions and classes, it is more efficient to work this way.

■ **Note**   In general, name your imported modules and import only what you need; that is, avoid "import *".

CHAPTER 6

■ ■ ■

Object Orientation[1]

What Is Object Orientation?

The professional approach to programming has shifted away from designing systems with a hierarchy of features defined in functions toward an object-oriented (OO) approach. We look here at how Python fully supports object orientation.

In this book, we can only give a flavor of how objects are used. We work through an example and introduce some of the most basic concepts. We use some OO concepts in our explanation so you need a basic understanding of OO to work through this section.

In OO design, systems are composed of collaborating sets of well-defined objects. Rather than one piece of functionality making use of another function, one object sends a message to another object to achieve some goal. The message is in effect a function call, but the function (usually called a method) is associated with the object in question and the behavior of the method depends on the nature of the object.

You have already come across objects in many places. In fact, in Python everything is an object; we just haven't elaborated on this OO view of the world. For example, a string has several useful methods:

```python
newstring = text.upper()  # uppercase the string
newstring = text.lower()  # lowercase the string
newstring = text.split('\n')  # split lines
```

The string functions return a new variable—the new object—sometimes called an *instance*[2] of the string class. The object (the new string) is the output of the method called on the original string.

---

[1]Object orientation is a big topic. You can see an overview of OO programming at http://en.wikipedia.org/wiki/Object-oriented_programming.
[2]When you create a new object from a class definition, that object is sometimes called an instance and the create process called instantiation. We use the word *object,* though, in our description.

© Paul Gerrard 2016
P. Gerrard, *Lean Python*, DOI 10.1007/978-1-4842-2385-7_6

In more complex objects, the object itself has attributes or properties that we can set and get.[3] We might create a person object, for example. The functions or methods that a person object allows would include a new or create method as well as various set methods and get methods; for example:

```
fred=customer(name='Fred') # create new customer
fred.setAge(49)            # change age to 49
fred.gender='Male'         # Fred is male
cdate=fred.getCreateDate() # get the creation date
age = fred.getAge()        # get Fred's age
del fred                   # Fred no longer wanted ☹
```

In the preceding example, you can see there were some get and set methods that get and set Fred's attributes, like his age and creation date. His age and creation date cannot be accessed directly except through these simple get and set functions.

There was one attribute that could be examined directly, though: fred.gender. It wasn't a method because there were no parentheses associated when we referenced it. We can access that attribute directly and we can set it just like any other variable through an assignment.

Creating Objects Using Classes

In our Python code, a new object is defined by referring to a class. In the same way that we can create an int(), a list(), and str() types, we can define our own more complex objects using a class definition.

A class definition is a template for a new object. It defines the mechanism and data required to create a new instance of that class, its attributes (both private and public), and the methods that can be used to set and get attributes or change the state of the object.

Note that we are not recommending this as a perfect implementation of a person class; it is just an example to illustrate the use of class definitions, object attributes, and methods.

The module that defines the person class is people.py:

```
1    from datetime import datetime
2
3    class person(object):
4        "Person Class"
5        def __init__(self,name,age,parent=None):
6            self.name=name
7            self.age=age
8            self.created=datetime.today()
9            self.parent=parent
10           self.children=[]
```

---

[3]It is a design choice as to whether we hide attributes and make them available only through methods (private attributes) or expose them to the outside world (public).

```
11          print('Created',self.name,'age',self.age)
12
13      def setName(self,name):
14          self.name=name
15          print('Updated name',self.name)
16
17      def setAge(self,age):
18          self.age=age
19          print('Updated age',self.age)
20
21      def addChild(self,name,age):
22          child=person(name,age,parent=self)
23          self.children.append(child)
24          print(self.name,'added child',child.name)
25
26      def listChildren(self):
27          if len(self.children)>0:
28              print(self.name,'has children:')
29              for c in self.children:
30                  print('  ',c.name)
31          else:
32              print(self.name,'has no children')
33
34      def getChildren(self):
35          return self.children
```

- Line 1 imports the datetime and printing modules we'll need later.

- Line 3 starts the class definition. We have used the generic object type, but classes can subclassed and inherit the attributes and methods of another parent class.

- Lines 5 through 11 creates a new object. Python doesn't need a "new" method: When the object is created, Python looks for an __init__() method to initialize the object. The arguments passed through the creation call are used here to initialize the object attributes.[4]

- The two methods in lines 13 through 19 update the object attribute's name and age.

---

[4]Note that the first argument to all of the methods in the class is `'self'`, the object itself. This argument is used internally in the class and is not exposed to the code that calls these methods, as you'll see in the test that follows. The `"self."` attributes are public.

- In lines 21 through 24, the addChild method creates a new person who is a child of the current person. The children objects are stored in an attribute children, which is a list of the person objects for each child.

- In lines 26 through 32, the listChildren method prints out the names of the children for this person.

- In lines 34 and 35, the getChildren method returns a list containing the children of this person.

■ Note   Class methods would not normally print information messages to describe their behavior. This instrumentation code in the class is there to show what's going on inside.

We wrote a program that tests the person class called testpeople.py. To show the output inline, I pasted the code into the interpreter. The embedded comments should explain what's going on.

```
1    >>> from people import person
2    >>> #
3    ... #   create a new instance of class person
4    ... #   for Joe Bloggs, age 47
5    ... #
6    ... joe=person('Joe Bloggs',47)
7    Created Joe Bloggs age 47
8    >>> #
9    ... #   use the age attribute to verify
10   ... #   Joe's age
11   ... #
12   ... print("Joe's age is",joe.age)
13   Joe's age is 47
14   >>> print("Joe's full name is ",joe.name)
15   Joe's full name is  Joe Bloggs
16   >>> #
17   ... #   add children Dick and Dora
18   ... #
19   ... joe.addChild('Dick',7)
20   Created Dick age 7
21   Joe Bloggs added child Dick
22   >>> joe.addChild('Dora',9)
23   Created Dora age 9
24   Joe Bloggs added child Dora
25   >>> #
26   ... #   use the listChildren method to list them
27   ... #
28   ... joe.listChildren()
```

```
29  Joe Bloggs has children:
30      Dick
31      Dora
32  >>> #
33  ... #   get the list variable containing Joe's children
34  ... #
35  ... joekids=joe.getChildren()
36  >>> #
37  ... #   print Joe's details.
38  ... #   NB the vars() function lists the values
39  ... #   of the object attributes
40  ... #
41  ... print("** Joe's attributes **")
42  ** Joe's attributes **
43  >>> print(vars(joe))
44  {'age': 47, 'children': [<people.person object at 0x021B25D0>, <people.
    person object at 0x021B2610>], 'name': 'Joe Bloggs', 'parent': None,
    'created': datetime.datetime(2014, 4, 4, 8, 23, 5, 221000)}
45  >>> #
46  ... #   print the details of his children
47  ... #   from the list we obtained earlier
48  ... #
49  ... print("** Joe's Children **")
50  ** Joe's Children **
51  >>> for j in joekids:
52  ...     print(j.name,'attributes')
53  ...     print(vars(j))
54  ...
55  Dick attributes
56  {'age': 7, 'children': [], 'name': 'Dick', 'parent': <people.person
    object at 0x021B2590>, 'created': datetime.datetime(2014, 4, 4, 8, 23,
    5, 229000)}
57  Dora attributes
58  {'age': 9, 'children': [], 'name': 'Dora', 'parent': <people.person
    object at 0x021B2590>, 'created': datetime.datetime(2014, 4, 4, 8, 23,
    5, 231000)}
59  >>>
```

- Line 1 imports the module we need.

- Line 6 creates a person by the name of Joe Bloggs.

- Lines 12 through 15 print Joe Bloggs's details.

- Lines 19 through 24 add two children to Joe's record. Note that the person class adds new person objects for each child.

- Line 28 calls the joe.listChildren() method to list the details of Joe's children.

- Line 35 uses the `joe.getChildren()` method to obtain a list of Joe's children objects.

- Lines 41 through 43 use the `vars()` function to collect the attributes of the `joe` object. You can see all of the variables defined for the object, including a list of Joe's children.

- Lines 51 through 53 loop through the `joekids` list printing the attributes of the children objects.

The preceding narrative gives you a flavor of how OO works in the Python language. OO is a large and complex topic that requires careful explanation.[5]

---

[5]The Python implementation of OO differs in some respects from other languages such as Java, for example. Python has a rather more "relaxed" attitude to OO, which makes some things easier for the programmer, but does mean that the programmer needs to be a little more careful in his or her coding. It is up to you to decide which approach is best.

CHAPTER 7

■ ■ ■

Exception and Error Handling

Exceptions and Errors

Things can go wrong in your code for many reasons. One reason is that the programmer has written some code that is faulty. Faults, defects, and bugs are labels we put on aspects of our program code that are not quite right. Faults occur because we, as programmers, are not perfect. We are human and are always going to get some things wrong. Early on in your programming career, you will learn that all is not plain sailing.[1]

Sometimes, you can control the input data and behavior of your programs, but the sheer number of ways in which your code can be dealt a curveball overwhelms your ability to deal with them. Out of this challenge came the approach called *defensive programming*.[2]

Defensive programming isn't a timid approach or lackluster attitude. It is a discipline that tackles the possibility of failure head on. A significant part of this discipline is the effective implementation of error and exception handling.

Let's look at an example. Suppose you had some code that implemented the division operation such as this:

```
quotient = a / b
```

What could possibly go wrong? Well the obvious problem occurs if the value of b is zero. What would we see?

```
>>> quotient = 73 / 0.0
Traceback (most recent call last):
  File "<stdin>", line 1, in <module>
ZeroDivisionError: float division by zero
>>>
```

---

[1] It could be said you don't learn by getting things right. You only learn from your mistakes. You are going to make a lot of mistakes; that's not the problem. The problem comes if you do not learn from them. A mantra that you might learn from is, "Fail Fast!" and learn from failure.
[2] See http://en.wikipedia.org/wiki/Defensive_programming.

© Paul Gerrard 2016
P. Gerrard, *Lean Python*, DOI 10.1007/978-1-4842-2385-7_7

The text ZeroDivisionError: float division by zero is what we are interested in. The Python interpreter raises an error ZeroDivisionError and provides an error message, albeit a rather terse one.

If this code fragment was in the middle of a program, the program would fail and terminate. That's not of much use to us if we want the program to handle the error and move on to the next calculation. We use the term *error handling* or more often, *exception handling*, to refer to how we do this.

Python has many built-in exception types—ZeroDivisionError is just one of them—and we can trap these occurrences and deal with this in our code. Here's an example program division.py:

```
1    print('Input two numbers. the first will be divided by the second')
2
3    afirst = input('first number:')
4    first=float(afirst)
5    asecond = input('second number:')
6    second = float(asecond)
7
8    quotient = first / second
9    print('Quotient first/second = ',quotient)
```

If you run this, enter say, 1 and 2 you get a result of 0.5, no problem. If you enter 1 and 0, you get the ZeroDivisionError message again.

Here's a new version of the program, divisionHandled.py.

```
1    print('Input two numbers. The first will be divided by the second')
2
3    afirst = input('1st number:')
4    asecond = input('2nd number:')
5
6    try:
7        first=float(afirst)
8        second = float(asecond)
9        quotient = first / second
10       print('Quotient 1st/2nd = ',quotient)
11   except Exception as diag:
12       print(diag.__class__.__name__,':',diag)
```

In this case, we have enclosed some of the code (the two text-to-float number conversions and the division) inside a try: clause on line 6. If any code inside the try: clause raises an error, it is trapped by the except: clause on line 11.

The except: clause identifies an exception type and optionally, a variable into which the exception data is stored. Exception is the top-level class for error type so it captures all errors. In the except code block, the code prints the diag.__class__.__name__ attribute, which names the error type.

So far, so good. If you play with this program you can try entering poor data, as shown here.

```
D:\LeanPython\programs>python divisionHandled.py
Input two numbers. The first will be divided by the second
1st number:
2nd number:
ValueError : could not convert string to float:

D:\LeanPython\programs>python divisionHandled.py
Input two numbers. The first will be divided by the second
1st number:1
2nd number:0
ZeroDivisionError : float division by zero
```

In the first run, the float conversion code fails. We know it is the first conversion by looking at the code, but an end user who didn't know the code might get confused. In general, therefore, it is recommended that:

- We handle particular errors rather than have a catch-all.

- Give each section of code its own exception handler to localize the error.

Here is the final version of our fully error-handled code: divisionHandledV2.py.

```
1   print('Input two numbers. The first will be divided by the second')
2
3   afirst = input('1st number:')
4   try:
5     first=float(afirst)
6     asecond = input('2nd number:')
7     try:
8       second = float(asecond)
9       try:
10        quotient = first / second
11        print('Quotient 1st/2nd = ',quotient)
12      except ZeroDivisionError as diag:
13        print(diag,': 2nd number must be non-zero')
14    except ValueError as diag:
15      print(diag,'2nd number')
16  except ValueError as diag:
17      print(diag,'1st number')
```

The slightly tricky part is that it is hard to know what error types will occur until you test for them, so the general approach might be this:

- First, capture all exceptions in places where you expect them to occur.

- Second, test for all the exceptions you can think of, trigger them, and make a note where they occur.

- For each exception type you find, create an exception clause specific to that exception.

By the way, note that it is possible to trap multiple exception types if you put them in a tuple; for example:

```
except (ValueError, ZeroDivisionError) [as e]:
```

The obvious alternative to handling errors that occur is to be more stringent on the validation of input data. In the preceding example, it might be a better alternative. In some circumstances, though, the exception cannot be checked for ahead of time because the data values that cause the exception are the result of intermediate calculations that might not be easily predicted.

The range of exception types is large. They cover things like type conversions, arithmetic, file I/O, database access, dictionary and list element violations, and so on. The full list is presented in the Appendix.

CHAPTER 8

■ ■ ■

Testing Your Code

Modularizing Code and Testing It[1]

So far, we have explained how to make use of the features of Python to create software that has some purpose and hopefully, value. When you write a little code, the natural thing to do then is to try it out, or test it.

The programs I have used to illustrate Python features run without any intervention, or require some user input via the input() function. As you get better at programming, you will become more ambitious and create larger programs. Then you realize that testing becomes more difficult, and more important. Splitting programs into functions and modules will make testing and debugging easier, as I said earlier.

Test-Driven Development

As your programs get bigger and more complicated, the chances of making a mistake or making a change that has an unwanted side effect increase. Should we run all of our previous tests every time we make a change then? It would be helpful, but doesn't the thought of running the same tests again and again bore you? Of course it might.

The test-driven development (TDD) approach for programming is gaining popularity. This is how it works:

- Developers write their (automated) tests first, before they write code.

- They run their tests and watch them fail, then add or correct code to make them pass.

- When their tests pass, they look for opportunities to improve the design of their code. Can you think of why?

TDD might not always be the best approach, but when it comes to writing larger programs it is best to modularize your code. When it comes to writing and testing classes and functions, using a unit test framework to create automated tests makes a lot of sense.

---

[1]Most programs are split into modules that are separately tested by the programmer. This testing is usually called unit or component testing.

© Paul Gerrard 2016
P. Gerrard, *Lean Python*, DOI 10.1007/978-1-4842-2385-7_8

The unittest Framework

In this chapter, I provide a brief introduction of how the unittest framework [20] can be used to test Python modules.

Suppose we need to write a function that performs simple arithmetic. The function is passed two numbers and an operator, which could be any of '+', '-', '*', or '/' to simulate addition, subtraction, multiplication, or division. It is as simple as that. Our function call might look like this:

```
result, msg = calc(12.34, '*', 98.76)
```

result would be the outcome of the calculation, or None if an error occurred. msg would contain a string version of the result or an error message if the calculation fails for some reason.

The line of code that called the calc function in this example looks like a test doesn't it? It is, except we haven't checked that the outputs (result and msg) are correct. In this case we would expect that:

- result would have the value 1218.6984.

- msg would have the value '1218.6984'.

Here is a possible implementation of the calc function in file calc.py:

```
def calc(a, op, b):

    if op not in '+-/*':
        return None, 'Operator must be +-/*'

    try:
        if op=='+':
            result=a+b
        elif op=='-':
            result=a-b
        elif op=='/':
            result=a/b
        else:
            result=a*b
    except Exception as e:
        return None,e.__class__.__name__

    return result,str(result)
```

The calc function does very little checking. It does no checking of the numeric values of the two number arguments a and b. After that, it attempts the calculation but traps any exceptions that occur, passing the name of the exception back in msg.

Now, to create a set of tests for the calc function, we have created a testcalc.py file as follows:

```
1   import unittest
2   import calc
3   #
4   #   define the test class
5   #
6   class testCalc(unittest.TestCase):
7
8       def testSimpleAdd(self):
9           result,msg = calc.calc(1,'+',1)
10          self.assertEqual(result,2.0)
11
12      def testLargeProduct(self):
13          result,msg = calc.calc(123456789.0, '*',987654321.0)
14          self.assertEqual(result, 1.2193263111263526e+17)
15
16      def testDivByZero(self):
17          result,msg = calc.calc(6,'/',0.0)
18          self.assertEqual(msg,'ZeroDivisionError')
19  #
20  #   create the test suite
21  #
22  TestSuite = unittest.TestSuite()
23  #
24  #   add tests to the suite
25  #
26  TestSuite.addTest(testCalc("testSimpleAdd"))
27  TestSuite.addTest(testCalc("testLargeProduct"))
28  TestSuite.addTest(testCalc("testDivByZero"))
29  #
30  #   create the test runner
31  #
32  runner = unittest.TextTestRunner()
33  #
34  #   execute the tests
35  #
36  runner.run(TestSuite)
```

- Line 1 imports the unittest module that we will use to test the calc function.

- Line 2 imports the calc module (the module to be tested).

- Line 6 defines the class (testCalc) that defines the tests.

- Lines 8 through 18 define three tests. The format of each is similar.

  - Each test has a unique name (normally test...).

  - It calls the function to be tested in some way.

  - It performs an assertion to check correctness (we cover assertions further later).

- Line 22 defines the test suite that will be run.

- Lines 26 through 28 add tests to the test suite (note that we can create multiple test suites with different selections of test).

- Line 32 defines the test runner.

- Line 36 runs the tests.

When we run the test we get this:

```
D:\LeanPython\programs>python testcalc.py
...
----------------------------------------------------------
Ran 3 tests in 0.001s

OK
```

The three dots appear as you run the tests, and represent the successful execution of each test. If a test had failed, we would have seen a Python error message indicating the exception and line number in the program where the failure occurred.

All this code just to run a few tests might seem a little excessive. Perhaps it looks a bit wordy, but there is purpose in each call. Note, however, that once it is set up, if I want to add a new tests, I create a new test call (e.g., lines 8–10) and add the test to the suite (e.g., line 26). Once you are set up, therefore, creating large numbers of tests is easy. The calc function is a rather simplistic example. More realistic (and complex) classes and functions sometimes require 20 or 30 or even hundreds of tests.

■ **Note** Programmers who offer their modules as open-source libraries often include a large suite of tests with their modules.[2]

---

[2]If they don't, perhaps their modules should be avoided.

Assertions

The key to good testing is the choice of inputs or stimuli applied to your code (the function call; e.g., line 9) and the check that is performed on the outcome. The checks are implemented as assertions. The `unittest` module provides around 20 different assertion variations. Examples include the following:

- `assertEquals`. This variation asserts exact equality between two values (the result and your predicted result).

- `assertTrue`. Is an expression true?

- `assertIn`. Is a value in a sequence?

- `assertGreaterEqual`. Is one value greater than or equal to another?

More Complex Test Scenarios

The `unittest` framework has many more features. Examples are `setup()` and `teardown()` methods in the `TestCase` class. These methods are called automatically, just before and just after each test case, to perform a standard setup (of variables, data, or the environment) to allow each test to run correctly. The teardown process tidies up after the test (if necessary).

■ **Note**　We have now covered the basic elements of the Python language and explored the `unittest` module for testing. Now, let's look at using some popular libraries to do something useful.

CHAPTER 9

■ ■ ■

Accessing the Web[1]

Python has standard libraries that enable programmers to write both clients and servers that both use and implement Internet services such as electronic mail, File Transfer Protocol (FTP), and, of course, web sites.

In this chapter we look at how it is possible to use Python to access web sites and services. Suppose you wanted to download a page from a web site and save the HTML that was retrieved. The user needs to enter a URL for the site. Perhaps you want to be able to add a query string to the URL to pass data to the request, and you want to then display the response or save it to disk.

You would design your program to work in stages, of course:

1. Ask the user for a URL.

2. Ask for the query string to append to the URL.

3. Ask whether to save to disk.

The listing of program webtest.py is shown here.

```
1    import requests
2    from urllib.parse import urlparse
3
4    url=input('Web url to fetch:')
5    urlparts=urlparse(url)
6    if urlparts[0]=='':
7        url=''.join(('http://',url))
8
9    qstring=input('Enter query string:')
10   if len(qstring)>0:
11       url='?'.join((url,qstring))
12
13   save=input('Save downloaded page to disk [y/n]?')
14
15   print('Requesting',url)
16
```

---

[1]Some familiarity with the operation of web servers, browsers, and HTML is assumed in this chapter.

© Paul Gerrard 2016
P. Gerrard, *Lean Python*, DOI 10.1007/978-1-4842-2385-7_9

```
17  try:
18      response = requests.get(url)
19      if save.lower()=='y':
20          geturl=response.url
21          urlparts=urlparse(geturl)
22          netloc=urlparts[1]
23          if len(netloc)==0:
24              fname='save.html'
25          else:
26              fname='.'.join((netloc,'html'))
27          print('saving to',fname,'...')
28          fp=open(fname,'w')
29          fp.write(response.text)
30          fp.close()
31      else:
32          print(response.text)
33  except Exception as e:
34      print(e.__class__.__name__,e)
```

Let's walk through this program.[2]

- Lines 1 and 2 import required modules (requests and urlparse).

- Lines 4 through 7 get a URL from the user. If the user doesn't include the http:// part of the URL, the program adds the prefix.

- Lines 10 through 12 ask the user for a query string and append it to the URL with a ? character.

- Lines 14 through 16 ask the user if he or she wants to save the output to a file, then print the full URL to be requested.

- Lines 18 through 40 do most of the work; any exception is trapped by lines 34 and 35.

- Line 19 gets the URL and saves the response in response.

- Lines 20 through 31 create a file name based on the URL to the web site (or uses save.html) and saves the output to that file.

- Line 33 prints the response content to the screen.

When I ran this program, this is what I saw:

```
D:\LeanPython\programs>python webtest.py
Web url to fetch:uktmf.com
Enter query string:q=node/5277
Save downloaded page to disk [y/n]?y
```

---

[2]Yes, it's a program, the first that really does something you might actually find useful.

```
Requesting http://uktmf.com?q=node/5277
saving to uktmf.com.html ...

d:\LeanPython\programs>
```

The contents of the downloaded page were saved in uktmf.com.html.

The requests library is very flexible in that you can access the HTTP "post" verb using requests.post().

You can provide data to post commands as follows:

```
data = {'param1': 'value 1','param2': 'value 2'}
response = request.post(url,data=data)
```

Where web sites or web services require it, you can provide credentials for authentication and obtain the content as JSON data. You can provide custom headers to requests and see the headers returned in the response easily, too.

The requests module can be used to test web sites and web services quite comprehensively.

CHAPTER 10

Searching

Searching for Strings

Searching for text in strings is a common activity and the built-in string function find() is all you need for simple searches. It returns the position (offset) of the find or −1 if not found.

```
>>> txt="The quick brown fox jumps over the lazy dog"
>>> txt.find('jump')
20
>>> txt.find('z')
37
>>> txt.find('green')
-1
```

More Complex Searches

There are often circumstances when the search is not so simple. Rather than a simple string, we need to look for a pattern and extract the information we really want from the matched text. Suppose for example, we wanted to extract all the URLs in links on a web page. Here are some example lines of HTML text from a real web page.

```
1    <link rel="alternate" type="application/rss+xml" title="RSS: 40 newest
     packages" href="https://pypi.python.org/pypi?:action=packages_rss"/>
2    <link rel="stylesheet" media="screen" href="/static/styles/screen-
     switcher-default.css" type="text/css"/>
3    <li><a class="" href="/pypi?%3Aaction=browse">Browse packages</a>
     </li>
4    <li><a href="http://wiki.python.org/moin/CheeseShopTutorial">PyPI
     Tutorial</a></li>
```

There is quite a lot going on in the text here.

- Line 1 refers to an RSS feed.

- Line 2 has an href attribute, but it refers to a Cascading Style Sheets (CSS) file, not a link.

© Paul Gerrard 2016
P. Gerrard, *Lean Python*, DOI 10.1007/978-1-4842-2385-7_10

- Line 3 is a true link but the URL is relative; it doesn't contain the web site part of the URL.

- Line 4 is a link to an external site.

How can we hope to use some software to find the links that we care about? Well, this is where regular expressions come in.

Introducing Regular Expressions[1]

Regular expressions[2] are a way of using pattern matching to find the text we are interested in. Not only are patterns matched, but the re module can extract the data we *really* want out of the matched text.

Many more examples could be written, and in fact there are whole books written about regular expressions (e.g., [16], [17]). There are many web sites, but the most useful is probably http://www.regular-expressions.info.

■ **Note**   A regex is a string containing both text and special characters that define a pattern that the re functions can use for matching.

Simple Searches

The simplest regex is a text string that you want to find in another string, as shown in Table 10-1.

Table 10-1. *Finding a Simple String*

Regex	String Matched
jumps	jumps
The Queen	The Queen
Pqr123	Pqr123

Using Special Characters

There are special characters, listed in Table 10-2, that influence how the match is to be performed.

---

[1]The full documentation of the Python re module can be found at https://docs.python.org/3/library/re.html. Regular expressions are an advanced topic in any programming language.
[2]Often, regular expression is shortened to regex.

Table 10-2. Using Special Characters

Symbols	Description	Example
literal	Match a literal string	Jumps
re1|re2	Match string re1 OR re2	Yes|No
.	Match any single character (except \n)	J.mps
^	Match start of string	^The
$	Match end of string	well$
*	Match 0 or more occurrences of preceding regex	[A-Z]*
+	Match 1 or more occurrences of preceding regex	[A-Z]+
?	Match 0 or 1 occurrences of preceding regex	[a-z0-9]?
{m,n}	Match between m and n occurrences of the preceding regex (n optional)	[0-9]{2,4}
[...]	Match any character from character class	[aeiou]
[x-y]	Match any character from range	[0-9],[A-Za-z]
[^...]	Do not match any character from character class	[^aeiou]

There are a number of special characters, listed in Table 10-3, that can be matched, too.

Table 10-3. Searching with Special Characters

Special Character	Description	Example
\d	Match any decimal digit	BBC\d
\w	Match any alphanumeric character	Radio\w+
\s	Match any whitespace character	The\sBBC

Table 10-4 gives some examples of regular expressions and the strings that they would match.

Table 10-4. Regular Expressions and Matching Strings

Regex	String(s) Matched
smith|jones	smith, jones
UNE..O	Any two characters between UN and O; e.g., UNESCO, UNEzyO, UNE99O
^The	Any string that starts with The
end$	Any string that ends with end
c[aiou]t	cat, cit, cot, cut
[dg][io][gp]	dig, dip, dog, dop, gig, gip, gog, gop
[a-d][e-i]	2 chars a/b/c/d followed by e/f/g/h/i

■ **Note**   Regexes can use any combination of text and special characters, so they can look extremely complicated sometimes. Start simple.

Finding Patterns in Text

Finding substrings in text is fine, but often we want to find patterns in text, rather than literal strings. Suppose we wanted to extract numeric values, phone numbers, or web site URLs from text. How do we do that? This is where the real power of regular expressions lies.

Here is an example regex:

```
\s[A-Z0-9._%+-]+@[A-Z0-9.-]+\.[A-Z]{2,4}[\s]
```

Can you guess what it might find? It is a regex for finding e-mail addresses in text. At first glance, this looks pretty daunting, so let's break it down into its constituent parts.[3] First, the regex refers only to uppercase letters (to reduce the length of the regex), so this assumes that the string to be searched has already been uppercased.

There are six elements to this regex:

1	\s	Leading whitespace
2	[A-Z0-9._%+-]+	One or more characters
3	@	@ character
4	[A-Z0-9.-]+	A-Z, 0-9.-
5	\.	Dot character
6	[A-Z]{2,4}	2 to 4 text characters
7	[\s\.]	Whitespace or full stop

Obviously, you need to know the rules for the pattern you search for and there are specific rules for the construction of e-mail addresses.

Here is the file `remail.py`.

```
1    import re          # The RegEx library
2    #
3    # our regular expression (to find e-mails)
4    # and text to search
5    #
6    regex = '\s[A-Z0-9._%+-]+@[A-Z0-9.-]+\.[A-Z]{2,4}[\s]'
7    text="""This is some text with x@y.z embedded e-mails
8    that we'll use as@example.com
9    some lines have no email addresses
```

---

[3]Note that this e-mail finder regex is not perfect. It would not find an address at the start of a string and it would ignore e-mail addresses with more than four characters in the trailing element (e.g., '.mobile').

```
10   others@have.two valid email@addresses.com
11   The re module is awonderful@thing."""
12   print('** Search text ***\n'+text)
13   print('** Regex ***\n'+regex+'\n***')
14   #
15   #   uppercase our text
16   utext=text.upper()
17   #
18   #   perform a search (any emails found?)
19   s = re.search(regex,utext)
20   if s:
21       print('*** At least one email found "'+s.group()+'"')
22   #
23   #   now, find all matches
24   #
25   m = re.findall(regex,utext)
26   if m:
27       for match in m:
28           print('Match found',match.strip())
```

- Line 1 imports the modules we need.

- Lines 6 through 13 define the text string to search and the regex we will use, then print them both.

- Line 16 uppercases the text.

- Lines 19 through 21 perform the simple search for the first (any) e-mail and print the result. Note that a match contains leading and trailing whitespace.

- Lines 25 through 28 find all matches in the text and print the results.

Note that the regex matches the e-mail address and the whitespace boundaries. In Line 21 we print the match including the trailing newline, but in line 28 we strip off the spare characters.

What do we get when we run this code? Here is the result.

```
D:\LeanPython\programs\Python3>python remail.py
** Search text ***
This is some text with x@y.z embedded emails
that we'll use as@example.com
some lines have no email addresses
others@have.two valid email@addresses.com
The re module is awonderful@thing.
** Regex ***
\s[A-Z0-9._%+-]+@[A-Z0-9.-]+\.[A-Z]{2,4}[\s]
***
```

```
*** At least one email found " AS@EXAMPLE.COM
"
Match found AS@EXAMPLE.COM
Match found OTHERS@HAVE.TWO
Match found EMAIL@ADDRESSES.COM
```

Capturing Parentheses

One more aspect we should mention is the use of parentheses. They can be searched for, like any other character, but they can also be used to delineate substrings that are matched, and the re module can capture these substrings and place them in a list returned by the search process. These so-called capturing parentheses feature in the following example and provide the URLs we want to extract from a page of HTML.

Finding Links in HTML

The following program downloads a single web page using the urllib library. The text of the downloaded HTML content is then searched using a complicated regular expression that extracts text links and provides the URL and the text of the link as seen by the user.

This program is called regex.py.

```
1    import urllib.request
2    import re            # The RegEx library
3    #
4    #   this code opens a connection to the leanpy.com website
5    #
6    response = urllib.request.urlopen('http://leanpy.com')
7    data1 = str(response.read())             # put response text in data
8    #
9    #   our regular expression (to find links)
10   #
11   regex = '<a\s[^>]*href\s*=\s*\"([^\"]*)\"[^>]*>(.*?)</a>'
12   #
13   #   compile the regex and perform the match (find all)
14   #
15   pm = re.compile(regex)
16   matches = pm.findall(data1)
17   #
18   #   matches is a list
19   #   m[0] - the url of the link
20   #   m[1] - text associated with the link
21   #
22   for m in matches:
23       ms=''.join(('Link: "',m[0],'" Text: "',m[1],'"'))
24       print(ms)
```

The output of this program is shown here.

```
1   D:\LeanPython\programs>python re.py
2   200 OK
3   Link: "http://leanpy.com/" Text: "Lean Python"
4   Link: "#content" Text: "Skip to content"
5   Link: "http://leanpy.com/" Text: "Home"
6   Link: "http://leanpy.com/?page_id=33" Text: "About Lean Python"
7   Link: "http://leanpy.com/" Text: "<img src="http://leanpy.com/wp-
    content/uploads/2014/04/cropped-LeanPythonHeader.jpg" class="header-
    image" width="950" height="247" alt="" />"
8   Link: "http://leanpy.com/?p=1" Text: "The Lean Python Pocketbook"
9   Link: "http://leanpy.com/?p=1#respond" Text: "<span class="leave-
    reply">Leave a reply</span>"
10  Link: "http://leanpy.com/wp-content/uploads/2014/04/
    OnePieceCover1-e1396444631642.jpg" Text: "<img class="wp-image-17
    alignleft" alt="OnePieceCover" src="http://leanpy.com/wp-content/
    uploads/2014/04/OnePieceCover1-e1396444631642-633x1024.jpg" width="305"
    height="491" />"
11  Link: "http://leanpy.com/?cat=3" Text: "Lean Python Book"
12  Link: "http://leanpy.com/?tag=book" Text: "Book"
13  Link: "http://leanpy.com/?p=1" Text: "<time class="entry-date"
    datetime="2014-04-02T12:06:06+00:00">April 2, 2014</time>"
14  Link: "http://leanpy.com/?author=1" Text: "paulg"
15  Link: "http://leanpy.com/?p=1" Text: "The Lean Python Pocketbook"
16  Link: "http://leanpy.com/?cat=3" Text: "Lean Python Book"
17  Link: "http://leanpy.com/wp-login.php?action=register" Text: "Register"
18  Link: "http://leanpy.com/wp-login.php" Text: "Log in"
19  Link: "http://leanpy.com/?feed=rss2" Text: "Entries <abbr title="Really
    Simple Syndication">RSS</abbr>"
20  Link: "http://leanpy.com/?feed=comments-rss2" Text: "Comments <abbr
    title="Really Simple Syndication">RSS</abbr>"
21  Link: "http://wordpress.org/" Text: "WordPress.org"
22  Link: "http://wordpress.org/" Text: "Proudly powered by WordPress"
```

You can see that the program identifies all the links, but isn't yet as smart as we might like.

- *Line 4:* This link uses a bookmark to the same page.

- *Line 7:* The link text is actually an image (do we need to worry about that?).

Perhaps you could improve on the regex used, as an exercise.

CHAPTER 11

Databases[1]

Every application makes use of some form of (persistent) storage. We have looked at plain text files already. In this chapter we consider how a database, in particular a relational database, can be accessed and used by Python programs.

Python provides standard functions to access all of the popular databases. There are many open source and commercial database products and each one has its own adapter that allows Python to connect to and use data held in it. For our purposes, we use the SQLite database because it requires no other installed software.

SQLite

SQLite is a very lightweight serverless tool. The core Python product includes the SQLite adapter, allowing us to demonstrate the most important database features. SQLite behaves in the same way as bigger systems, but has low (near-zero) administrative overhead. A consequence of this is that SQLite can be used for development or prototyping and migrating to a more sophisticated database can be done later. For our purposes, SQLite provides all the features we require.

Database Functions

These are the key SQLite database functions we will be using:

```
# open (or create) a database file and return
# the connection
conn = sqlite3.connect(filename)

# executes a SQL statement
conn.executescript(sql)

# return a cursor
cursor = conn.cursor()
```

---

[1]This chapter presumes a knowledge of the relational database model and simple Structured Query Language (SQL) commands.

© Paul Gerrard 2016
P. Gerrard, *Lean Python*, DOI 10.1007/978-1-4842-2385-7_11

```
# execute the SQL query that returns rows of data
cursor.execute(sql)

# returns the data as a list of rows
rows = cursor.fetchall()
```

Connecting and Loading Data into SQLite

Here is an example program that creates a new database, a single table, inserts some data, performs a query, and attempts to insert a duplicate row (dbcreate.py).

```
1    import os
2    import sqlite3
3
4    db_filename='mydatabase.db'
5    #
6    #   if DB exists - delete it
7    #
8    exists = os.path.exists(db_filename)
9    if exists:
10       os.unlink(db_filename)
11   #
12   #   connect to DB (create it if it doesn't exist)
13   #
14   conn = sqlite3.connect(db_filename)
15   #
16   #   create a table
17   #
18   schema="""create table person (
19     id integer primary key autoincrement not null,
20     name text not null,
21     dob   date,
22     nationality text,
23     gender text)
24     """
25   conn.executescript(schema)
26   #
27   # create some data
28   #
29   people="""insert into person (name, dob,nationality,gender)
30   values ('Fred Bloggs', '1965-12-25','British','Male');
31   insert into person (name, dob,nationality,gender)
32   values ('Santa Claus', '968-01-01','Lap','Male');
33   insert into person (name, dob,nationality,gender)
34   values ('Tooth Fairy', '1931-03-31','American','Female');
35   """
36   conn.executescript(people)
```

```
37  #
38  #    execute a query
39  #
40  cursor = conn.cursor()
41  cursor.execute("select id, name, dob,nationality,gender from person")
42  for row in cursor.fetchall():
43      id, name, dob,nationality,gender = row
44      print("%3d %15s %12s %10s %6s" % (id, name, dob,nationality,gender))
45  #
46  #    attempt to insert a person with no name
47  #
48  try:
49      dupe="insert into person (id, dob,nationality,gender) \
50      values (1,'1931-03-31','American','Female');"
51      conn.executescript(dupe)
52  except Exception as e:
53      print('Cannot insert record',e.__class__.__name__)
```

- Lines 1 and 2 import the modules we need.

- Lines 4 through 10 delete an old database file if one exists (be careful not to use the database created in this program for anything useful!).

- Line 14 creates the database file.

- In lines 18 through 25, the schema is a set of commands (a SQL script) that will create a new table.

- Line 26 executes the SQL script to create the new table.

- In lines 29 through 36 a new script is defined that includes the SQL commands to insert three records in the new table.

- Line 37 executes the script.

- In lines 40 through 44, to execute a query, you need to create a cursor, then execute the query using that cursor. This establishes the query content but doesn't fetch the data. The cursor.fetchall() provides an iterable list of rows that are assigned to named variables, which are then printed.

- Lines 48 through 53 set up an insert of a row and the try...except clauses catch errors on the insert. The insert SQL omits the name field deliberately to trigger an exception.

The output from this program is shown hee.

```
D:\LeanPython\programs>python dbcreate.py
  1     Fred Bloggs    1965-12-25    British    Male
  2     Santa Claus     968-01-01        Lap    Male
  3     Tooth Fairy    1931-03-31   American  Female
Cannot insert record IntegrityError
```

The exception caused by the insert statement on line 52 is triggered because the name field is not supplied (and must be not null).

In the following listing (dbupdate.py), we are passing two arguments to the program and using those in a SQL update command to change the nationality of a person.

```
1   import sqlite3
2   import sys
3   #
4   #    arguments from command line
5   #    use: python dbupdate.py    1   Chinese
6   #
7   db_filename = 'mydatabase.db'
8   inid = sys.argv[1]
9   innat = sys.argv[2]
10  #
11  #    execute update using command-line arguments
12  #
13  conn = sqlite3.connect(db_filename)
14  cursor = conn.cursor()
15  query = "update person set nationality = :nat where id = :id"
16  cursor.execute(query, {'id':inid, 'nat':innat})
17  #
18  #    list the persons to see changes
19  #
20  cursor.execute("select id, name, dob,nationality,gender from person")
21  for row in cursor.fetchall():
22      id, name, dob,nationality,gender = row
23      print("%3d %15s %12s %10s %6s" % (id, name, dob,nationality,gender))
```

- Lines 8 and 9 get the data from the command line: inid and innat.

- Lines 13 through 16 do most of the work. Lines 13 and 14 set up the cursor. Line 15 is SQL as before, but the values to be used for the fields in the SQL (id and nat) are parameterized using the colon notation (:id and :nat). Line 16 executes the query and provides the actual values of the parameters using a dictionary as the second argument to the call {'id':inid, 'nat':innat}.

The output is shown here.

```
D:\LeanPython\programs>python dbupdate.py 1 Chinese
   1    Fred Bloggs    1965-12-25    Chinese    Male
   2    Santa Claus     968-01-01        Lap    Male
   3    Tooth Fairy    1931-03-31   American  Female
```

The colon notation and dictionary can be used to parameterize any SQL call.

CHAPTER 12

■ ■ ■

What Next?

In this little book, I have introduced the core Python features that I use in my own Python development. If you worked through all the examples, experimented using the interactive interpreter, and played with the example programs, you will have a pretty good grasp of the most fundamental elements of this wonderful programming language.

Other aspects of Python might seem fairly mysterious, though. The sections on regular expressions, web applications, and SQLite are intended only to whet your appetite to learn more.

If, like me, you get the programming bug, there will be no stopping you from exploring the language and what you can do with it. If you are an experienced programmer using another language, I hope you appreciate how Python works and the ease with which you can write code. You might even think of abandoning your old language in favor of Python. Some of you might have seen enough. Programming, Python, and all that nonsense might not be for you. You suspected this before and, well, at least you know for sure now.

If you do choose to go further, here is some advice:

1. Buy a good language reference book or familiarize yourself with the online Python references given in the Appendix.

2. Explore the PyPI resource. Whatever you want to do in code, someone else will have created a library that will make your life much easier. Take advantage of that.

3. Practice. It is as simple as that. Like spoken language and many other skills, if you don't use it you will lose it. If you aren't using Python for work this week, then have fun with it instead.

If you go further with Python, I know you'll have fun!

Appendices

References
Web[1]

1. http://www.artima.com/intv/pythonP.html. An interview with Guido van Rossum, the inventor of Python.

2. http://en.wikipedia.org/wiki/Python_(programming_language). The Wikipedia entry for the Python language.

3. http://web2py.com. The Web2py web development framework by Massimo De Pierro.

4. http://legacy.python.org/dev/peps/pep-0008/. A (PEP 8) style guide for Python code.

5. http://legacy.python.org/dev/peps/pep-0020/. The Zen of Python.

6. https://wiki.python.org/moin/Python2orPython3. Should I use Python 2 or Python 3?

7. https://pypi.python.org/pypi. Python Package Index.

8. https://docs.python.org/3/using/cmdline.html. Using the Python command-line environment.

9. http://www.python.org. The official site for the Python language.

10. https://docs.python.org/. Python standard documentation.

11. https://docs.python.org/3/library/index.html. Python Standard Library.

12. http://legacy.python.org/dev/peps/pep-0020/. The Zen of Python (2014).

Books

13. *Core Python Programming,* Wesley Chun.

14. *The Python Standard Library by Example,* Doug Hellmann.

15. *Python Cookbook,* Alex Martelli, David Ascher, and Anna Martelli Ravenscroft.

---

[1]These URLs worked at the time of publication but are subject to change.

16. *Mastering Python Regular Expressions*, Felix Lopez and Victor Romero.

17. *Mastering Regular Expressions*, Jeffrey Friedl.

Tools

18. Visual CESIL: `http://www.obelisk.me.uk/cesil/` (2016).

19. PIP Installer: `http://www.pip-installer.org/` (2014).

20. The Python unittest framework: `https://docs.python.org/3.4/library/unittest.html`.

Python Built-In Exceptions Hierarchy[2]

In Chapter 7, we described how Python manages exceptions. We introduced a few exception types there, but here is the full list.

```
BaseException
+-- SystemExit
+-- KeyboardInterrupt
+-- GeneratorExit
+-- Exception
     +-- StopIteration
     +-- StandardError
     |    +-- BufferError
     |    +-- ArithmeticError
     |    |    +-- FloatingPointError
     |    |    +-- OverflowError
     |    |    +-- ZeroDivisionError
     |    +-- AssertionError
     |    +-- AttributeError
     |    +-- EnvironmentError
     |    |    +-- IOError
     |    |    +-- OSError
     |    |         +-- WindowsError (Windows)
     |    |         +-- VMSError (VMS)
     |    +-- EOFError
     |    +-- ImportError
     |    +-- LookupError
     |    |    +-- IndexError
     |    |    +-- KeyError
     |    +-- MemoryError
```

---

[2]Extracted from `https://docs.python.org/3/library/exceptions.html`.

```
    |     +-- NameError
    |     |    +-- UnboundLocalError
    |     +-- ReferenceError
    |     +-- RuntimeError
    |     |    +-- NotImplementedError
    |     +-- SyntaxError
    |     |    +-- IndentationError
    |     |         +-- TabError
    |     +-- SystemError
    |     +-- TypeError
    |     +-- ValueError
    |          +-- UnicodeError
    |               +-- UnicodeDecodeError
    |               +-- UnicodeEncodeError
    |               +-- UnicodeTranslateError
    +-- Warning
         +-- DeprecationWarning
         +-- PendingDeprecationWarning
         +-- RuntimeWarning
         +-- SyntaxWarning
         +-- UserWarning
         +-- FutureWarning
                   +-- ImportWarning
                   +-- UnicodeWarning
                   +-- BytesWarning
```

■ ■ ■

Further Information

Contacting the Author

Should you have any questions or wish to discuss any of the issues raised in this book, or perhaps if would like help in improving development or testing in your organization, please feel free to contact me.

E-mail: paul@gerrardconsulting.com

Are You Interested in Training?

Gerrard Consulting has provided training courses since 1992.

Learning Python (1- or 2-day course)

You will learn and understand the basic constructs of Python and some fundamentals of software design.

After the course, you will

- Understand how a program can be constructed.

- Appreciate some of the complexities of software and difficulties of development.

- Be familiar with the concepts of variables, decisions, loops, input, and output.

- Recognize the structure of a Python program and how to read code.

- Have some useful text file and web testing utilities.

Drop me an e-mail at paul@gerrardconsulting.com if you are interested.

© Paul Gerrard 2016
P. Gerrard, *Lean Python*, DOI 10.1007/978-1-4842-2385-7

Online Training

There are a host of online resources aimed at helping you get to grips with Python. Just search for "learn python" or "python tutorial" and you'll find lots of examples.

leanpy.com

Visit the leanpy.com web site. I'm happy to answer questions about the book or Python.

Index

© Paul Gerrard 2016
P. Gerrard, *Lean Python*, DOI 10.1007/978-1-4842-2385-7

Get the eBook for only $4.99!

Why limit yourself?

Now you can take the weightless companion with you wherever you go and access your content on your PC, phone, tablet, or reader.

Since you've purchased this print book, we are happy to offer you the eBook for just $4.99.

Convenient and fully searchable, the PDF version enables you to easily find and copy code—or perform examples by quickly toggling between instructions and applications.

To learn more, go to http://www.apress.com/us/shop/companion or contact support@apress.com.